# Implementing Purchasing and Supply Chain Management

## Best Practices in Market Research

Nancy Nicosia, Nancy Y. Moore

Prepared for the United States Air Force

Approved for public release; distribution unlimited

**PROJECT AIR FORCE**

The research reported here was sponsored by the United States Air Force under Contract F49642-01-C-0003. Further information may be obtained from the Strategic Planning Division, Directorate of Plans, Hq USAF.

**Library of Congress Cataloging-in-Publication Data**

Nicosia, Nancy.
    Implementing purchasing and supply chain management : best practices in market research / Nancy Nicosia, Nancy Y. Moore.
      p. cm.
    "RAND Project Air Force."
    Includes bibliographical references.
    ISBN-13: 978-0-8330-3985-9 (pbk. : alk. paper)
    1. United States. Air Force—Procurement. 2. Marketing research—United States.  I. Moore, Nancy Y., 1947– . II. Title.

UG1123.N53 2006
358.4'162120973—dc22

               2006030994

The RAND Corporation is a nonprofit research organization providing objective analysis and effective solutions that address the challenges facing the public and private sectors around the world. RAND's publications do not necessarily reflect the opinions of its research clients and sponsors.

**RAND®** is a registered trademark.

Published 2006 by the RAND Corporation
1776 Main Street, P.O. Box 2138, Santa Monica, CA 90407-2138
1200 South Hayes Street, Arlington, VA 22202-5050
4570 Fifth Avenue, Suite 600, Pittsburgh, PA 15213-2665
RAND URL: http://www.rand.org/
To order RAND documents or to obtain additional information, contact
Distribution Services: Telephone: (310) 451-7002;
Fax: (310) 451-6915; Email: order@rand.org

# Preface

To achieve targets for increased aircraft availability with decreases in costs, the Air Force is implementing selected purchasing and supply management practices that are well-respected in the commercial sector. The implementation is currently focused on the establishment of commodity councils (or commodity teams)—teams of cross-functional Air Force personnel who have responsibility for developing and implementing proactive, tailored purchasing strategies for key groups of goods and services. The commodity councils must be equipped with the market research and analysis necessary to develop and implement strategic sourcing plans. They must be able to collect and analyze relevant data on the industry, market, and suppliers for their selected commodity groups. This kind of market research and analysis extends beyond the traditional activities of Air Force procurement personnel. To address this disparity, RAND Project AIR FORCE was asked to develop a guide to assist procurement personnel in their new market research efforts.

This monograph is based on our review of the relevant literature and a series of interviews with procurement professionals at commercial enterprises that are well-respected for their sourcing practices. The monograph is intended to serve two purposes. First, it provides some background information about market research and its relevance to commercial and Air Force purchasing activities. The monograph assumes some basic understanding of purchasing and supply management practices, but it also defines terms and concepts for the lay reader. Second, the monograph provides a summary of "how-to" guidance for Air Force commodity teams that are tasked with conducting market research. The monograph is ambitious in its goals, and our hope is that it will achieve those goals and thus prove both interesting and useful to a broad audience, including the reader who wants general information about market research *and* the practitioner who wants to know, "How do I begin?" The goal of this research is to help the Air Force achieve its ultimate goals—to improve aircraft availability with a reduction in costs.

This research was conducted as part of a larger study entitled "Best Practices for Purchasing and Supply Chain Management: Developing Effective Market Research Methods and Proactive Supply Strategies for Low Demand Items," sponsored by the U.S. Air Force Deputy Chief of Staff for Logistics, Installations, and Mission Support, Directorate of Transformation (USAF/A4I) and the Deputy Assistant Secretary (Contracting) (SAF/AQC), and conducted within the Resource Management Program of RAND Project AIR FORCE. Readers may also be interested in the following related RAND publications:

- *Air Force Service Procurement: Approaches for Measurement and Management,* Laura H. Baldwin, John A. Ausink, and Nancy Nicosia (MG-299-AF, 2005).
- *Air Force Procurement Workforce Transformation: Lessons from the Commercial Sector,* John A. Ausink, Laura H. Baldwin, and Christopher Paul (MG-214-AF, 2004).
- *Using a Spend Analysis to Help Identify Prospective Air Force Purchasing and Supply Management Initiatives: Summary of Selected Findings,* Nancy Y. Moore, Cynthia R. Cook, Clifford Grammich, and Charles Lindenblatt (DB-434-AF, 2004).
- *Implementing Best Purchasing and Supply Management Practices: Lessons from Innovative Commercial Firms,* Nancy Y. Moore, Laura H. Baldwin, Frank Camm, and Cynthia R. Cook (DB-334-AF, 2002).
- *Implementing Performance-Based Services Acquisition (PBSA): Perspectives from an Air Logistics Center and a Product Center,* John A. Ausink, Laura H. Baldwin, Sarah Hunter, and Chad Shirley (DB-388-AF, 2002).
- *Federal Contract Bundling: A Framework for Making and Justifying Decisions for Purchased Services,* Laura H. Baldwin, Frank Camm, and Nancy Y. Moore (MR-1224-AF, 2001).
- *Performance-Based Contracting in the Air Force: A Report on Experiences in the Field,* John A. Ausink, Frank Camm, and Charles Cannon (DB-342-AF, 2001).
- *Strategic Sourcing: Measuring and Managing Performance,* Laura H. Baldwin, Frank Camm, and Nancy Y. Moore (DB-287-AF, 2000).
- *Incentives to Undertake Sourcing Studies in the Air Force,* Laura H. Baldwin, Frank Camm, Edward G. Keating, and Ellen M. Pint (DB-240-AF, 1998).
- *Strategic Sourcing: Theory and Evidence from Economics and Business Management,* Ellen M. Pint and Laura H. Baldwin (MR-865-AF, 1997).

## RAND Project AIR FORCE

RAND Project AIR FORCE (PAF), a division of the RAND Corporation, is the U.S. Air Force's federally funded research and development center for studies and analyses. PAF provides the Air Force with independent analyses of policy alternatives affecting the development, employment, combat readiness, and support of current and future aerospace forces. Research is conducted in four programs: Aerospace Force Development; Manpower, Personnel, and Training; Resource Management; and Strategy and Doctrine.

Additional information about PAF is available on our Web site at http://www.rand.org/paf.

# Contents

**Preface** ........................................................................................... iii

**Figures** .......................................................................................... ix

**Tables** ........................................................................................... xi

**Interview Lessons** ....................................................................... xiii

**Summary** ....................................................................................... xv

**Acknowledgments** ....................................................................... xxi

**Abbreviations** ............................................................................ xxiii

CHAPTER ONE

**Introduction** ..................................................................................... 1

Market Research ................................................................................ 2

    What Is Market Research? .......................................................... 2

    Benefits of Market Research ....................................................... 2

Where to Look for Relevant Market Research Information .............. 3

Current Air Force Market Research ................................................. 3

Approach ............................................................................................ 4

    Literature Review ........................................................................ 4

    Interviews with Successful Commercial Enterprises .................. 4

About This Monograph ...................................................................... 5

    Key Terms and Concepts ............................................................ 5

    Organization of This Monograph ............................................. 5

CHAPTER TWO

**Focus Market Research Resources and Efforts Where They Are Most Needed** ..................... 9

Collect the Facts About the Enterprise .............................................. 9

    Understand Strategic Goals, Competencies, and Requirements ..... 9

    Analyze Spending ...................................................................... 10

    Develop (or Update) the Sourcing Strategy ............................. 10

Allocate Market Research Resources and Efforts to Maximize Rewards and Minimize Risks ....... 16

Summary ........................................................................................... 19

    Review: What to Do .................................................................. 19

    Where to Look for Relevant Information ................................. 19

**CHAPTER THREE**

**Analyze the Industry** ........................................................... 21

Assess How Competitive the Industry Is and How That Affects Sourcing ........................... 22

    Entry Barriers ........................................................... 24

    The Threat of Substitutes ........................................................... 27

    The Bargaining Power of Suppliers ........................................................... 28

    Rivalry Among Existing Suppliers ........................................................... 30

    Bargaining Power of Buyers ........................................................... 33

Benchmark the Industry Standards and Norms ........................................................... 36

    Industry Standards ........................................................... 36

    Industry Norms ........................................................... 38

Analyze Price and Cost ........................................................... 39

    Conducting a Should-Cost Analysis ........................................................... 39

    Conducting a Total-Cost Analysis ........................................................... 40

Investigate the Industry's Past and Anticipate the Future ........................................................... 44

    Looking Back at Trends ........................................................... 44

    Projecting the Future ........................................................... 44

Summary ........................................................... 46

    Review: What to Do ........................................................... 46

    Where to Look for Relevant Information ........................................................... 46

**CHAPTER FOUR**

**Identify Potential Suppliers** ........................................................... 47

Sources of Information ........................................................... 47

    Supplier Database ........................................................... 47

    Supplier Web Sites ........................................................... 49

    Supplier Catalogs ........................................................... 49

    Supplier Annual Reports ........................................................... 49

    Industry Web Sites ........................................................... 49

    Trade Registers and Directories ........................................................... 49

    Trade Journals ........................................................... 49

    Trade Associations ........................................................... 50

    Phone Directories ........................................................... 50

    Supplier Sales Personnel ........................................................... 50

    Professional Purchasing Organizations and Other Purchasing Professionals ........................................................... 50

    Enterprise Personnel (Corporate Knowledge) ........................................................... 50

Summary ........................................................... 51

    Review: What to Do ........................................................... 51

    Where to Look for Relevant Information ........................................................... 51

**CHAPTER FIVE**

**Evaluate Potential Suppliers**..................................................................... 53
Stage 1: Preliminary Analysis.................................................................... 54
Stage 2: Financial Analysis....................................................................... 56
Stage 3: Analyses of Performance, Cost, and Capabilities .............................. 57
    Performance Analyses ......................................................................... 57
    Cost Analyses.................................................................................... 59
    Capability Analyses............................................................................ 60
Stage 4: Evaluation Conference Between the Buyer and the Supplier ................. 63
Summary............................................................................................. 63
    Review: What to Do ........................................................................... 63
    Where to Look for Relevant Information.................................................. 64

**CHAPTER SIX**

**Manage the Supply Base**........................................................................... 65
Monitor Suppliers and the Industry ............................................................ 65
Developing Suppliers ............................................................................... 67
Summary............................................................................................. 68
    Review: What to Do ........................................................................... 68
    Where to Look for Relevant Information.................................................. 68

**CHAPTER SEVEN**

**Putting It All Together: Current Air Force Market Research and Next Steps** ...... 69
Current Air Force Market Research .............................................................. 69
Recommendations for the Air Force ............................................................ 70
    Improve Data Availability, Quality, and Utilization..................................... 70
    Provide Training for Commodity Teams .................................................. 71
    Ensure Management Support and Staff Buy In ......................................... 71

**APPENDIX**

A. **Interview Protocol**.............................................................................. 73
B. **The Sourcing Strategy** ........................................................................ 77
C. **Internet Sources of Information** ........................................................... 87
D. **Sources for Researching Financial Status**............................................... 93
E. **Supplier Evaluation Tools**................................................................... 95

**Bibliography**......................................................................................... 105

# Figures

2.1. Portfolio Analysis ................................................................. 18
3.1. Factors in an Industry's Competitive Structure ............................. 23
3.2. A TCO Analysis ................................................................... 42

# Tables

| | | |
|---|---|---:|
| 1.1. | Glossary | 6 |
| 2.1. | Pareto Analysis | 16 |
| 3.1. | Entry Barriers | 26 |
| 3.2. | Threat of Substitutes | 28 |
| 3.3. | Bargaining Power of Suppliers | 28 |
| 3.4. | Market Rivalry | 31 |
| 3.5. | Bargaining Power of Buyers | 34 |
| 3.6. | Industry Standards | 36 |
| 3.7. | Industry Norms | 38 |
| 3.8. | A Should-Cost Analysis | 40 |
| 3.9. | Example of a Should-Cost Buildup in Manufacturing | 41 |
| 5.1. | Sample Financial Indicators | 56 |
| 5.2. | Areas for Capability Analyses | 61 |
| B.1. | Sourcing Strategy Components | 78 |
| B.2. | Matrix Linking Supplier Relationship to the Operational Characteristics of the Purchase | 84 |
| C.1. | Online Sources of Information | 87 |
| D.1. | Sources of Financial Data | 93 |
| D.2. | Interpreting Key Financial Ratios | 94 |
| E.1. | Ratings for the Illustrative Plant Survey | 98 |
| E.2. | Initial Supplier Evaluation | 103 |

## Interview Lessons

Tracking Spend Comprehensively . . . . . . . . . . . . . . . . . . . . . . . . . . . . . . . . . . . . . . . . . . . 11
Proactive Buying Policies . . . . . . . . . . . . . . . . . . . . . . . . . . . . . . . . . . . . . . . . . . . . . . . . . . . 12
Ensuring Supply of Obsolete and Low-Demand Goods . . . . . . . . . . . . . . . . . . . . . 12
The Commodity Team as the One Face to the Supplier . . . . . . . . . . . . . . . . . . . . . . 13
Single Sourcing for Low-Demand Items . . . . . . . . . . . . . . . . . . . . . . . . . . . . . . . . . . . . 14
Number of Suppliers and Supply Base Rationalization . . . . . . . . . . . . . . . . . . . . . 14
Supporting Diversity Suppliers . . . . . . . . . . . . . . . . . . . . . . . . . . . . . . . . . . . . . . . . . . . . 15
Strategic Arrangements . . . . . . . . . . . . . . . . . . . . . . . . . . . . . . . . . . . . . . . . . . . . . . . . . . . 16
Total Cost of Ownership and Consolidation of Contracts . . . . . . . . . . . . . . . . . . 43
Sharing Information with Suppliers . . . . . . . . . . . . . . . . . . . . . . . . . . . . . . . . . . . . . . . . 45
Looking Beyond First-Tier Suppliers . . . . . . . . . . . . . . . . . . . . . . . . . . . . . . . . . . . . . . 54
Prequalified Suppliers . . . . . . . . . . . . . . . . . . . . . . . . . . . . . . . . . . . . . . . . . . . . . . . . . . . . . 55
Performance Data . . . . . . . . . . . . . . . . . . . . . . . . . . . . . . . . . . . . . . . . . . . . . . . . . . . . . . . . . 58
Scorecards for Potential Suppliers . . . . . . . . . . . . . . . . . . . . . . . . . . . . . . . . . . . . . . . . . 59
Supplier Attitude . . . . . . . . . . . . . . . . . . . . . . . . . . . . . . . . . . . . . . . . . . . . . . . . . . . . . . . . . . 62
Supplier Development . . . . . . . . . . . . . . . . . . . . . . . . . . . . . . . . . . . . . . . . . . . . . . . . . . . . . 67

# Summary

The U.S. Air Force is adopting widely accepted commercial "best practices" to change the way it purchases goods and services, with the goals of reducing costs and improving performance to better support its missions. Specifically, the Air Force wants to increase aircraft availability (i.e., the number of Air Force aircraft that are maintained and ready to fly at any time) by 20 percent over the next five years while at the same time reducing costs by 10 percent[1]—all in a changing security environment that requires the Air Force to be ready to respond to a variety of international and domestic threats and emergencies.

Part of the Air Force effort involves the establishment of "commodity councils" (or commodity teams), cross-functional teams of stakeholders who develop and implement Air Force–wide strategies for purchasing specific categories of commodities such as computers or medical supplies. Commodity councils will enable the Air Force to leverage its purchasing power and manage its contracts more effectively.

Commodity teams need information and analyses in order to do their jobs effectively. First, the commodity teams need information to help them understand their own enterprise (i.e., the Air Force) and develop purchasing strategies that are consistent with the enterprise's mission, culture, strategic goals, internal capabilities, budget, etc. Then, through market research, the councils need to understand the industry related to the required good or service, who the potential suppliers of the good or service are, how to select the best suppliers, and how to manage the enterprise-supplier relationship. Market research is essential to assembling and maintaining a supply base that best meets the Air Force's needs.

This monograph provides both background material about market research and an introductory "how-to" guide. Market research should be ongoing—in that it continues beyond initial supplier selection to supplier management and development. Clearly, however, the first iteration will be the most time intensive.

---

[1] These goals are from the Fiscal Year Defense Plan (fiscal year 11) U.S. Air Force Deputy Chief of Staff for Logistics, Installations, and Mission Support (AF/A4/7) goals (U.S. Air Force, 2005). "Stretch" goals for purchasing and supply chain management are a 20 percent increase in aircraft availability with a 20 percent decrease in costs.

## Focus Market Research Resources and Efforts Where They Are Most Needed

The first task for the commodity teams is not a core part of market research, but it is necessary before market research can be effective (pp. 9–19). The teams must understand various aspects of the Air Force itself before looking outward at the industry and potential suppliers. Information about the Air Force will help the commodity teams decide how to allocate costly market research efforts. For example, the commodity teams must understand the following:

- Strategic goals, competencies, and requirements:
  – Strategic goals—Air Force strategic goals include increasing aircraft availability at reduced costs; in the commercial sector, a goal might be to increase market share.
  – Core competencies—what can or should the enterprise produce itself and what should it buy?
  – Requirements—what goods and services are needed? What specifications and level of performance are necessary to achieve the enterprise's goals?
- Spend—a spend analysis explores the total amount the enterprise spends to obtain goods and services and analyzes expenditures by commodity, supplier, and other relevant categories. Two common tools are useful for analysis of the data and making informed decisions about allocating market research resources and efforts:
  – Pareto analysis groups goods and services into categories based on spend and volume.
  – Portfolio analysis focuses on vulnerability and value, quantifying the relative risks and rewards of each good or service and characterizing their importance to the enterprise.
- Sourcing strategy—the approach developed by the enterprise to procure a good or service. The four main elements of a sourcing strategy are:
  – the buying policy
  – the number of sources
  – the type of source
  – the nature of the enterprise-supplier relationship.

## Analyze the Industry

The first step in market research is to develop an understanding of the industry pertinent to the good or service (pp. 21–46).[2] This industry analysis touches upon factors that affect sourcing: the competitiveness of an industry, industry standards and norms, and costs. It is useful to start the market research process with this general overview of the industry and then work toward a more detailed investigation of the factors that are most relevant. The industry analysis will then also shape the identification, evaluation, and management of suppliers described in later chapters.

---

[2]  *Market* and *industry* are not synonymous. A supplier from another industry may offer a substitute product that would be in the "market." However, we will use the term *industry* here to encompass an industry and its substitutes in order to avoid confusion with the market research terminology.

First, the commodity team should assess how competitive an industry is and how that competitiveness affects sourcing. For example, if an industry report indicates that the industry is declining (e.g., the market is shrinking), then there should be competition among suppliers for remaining demand. This competition, in turn, should improve sourcing opportunities with respect to cost and other performance indicators. A declining industry may also involve increased risk of exit. The analysis should then examine more deeply which suppliers are most competitive and viable (i.e., those that have a limited risk of exit) and why. The analysis may reveal economies of scope—production synergies for suppliers who produce two or more related products—which are essential to lowering supplier costs and ensuring suppliers' long-term financial health. The enterprise may then identify and evaluate suppliers keeping in mind that those who produce multiple products may offer lower prices and may represent less supply risk.

Second, it is important that an industry analysis "benchmark"—identify and measure—industry standards and norms. Benchmarks are useful rules-of-thumb that can guide the sourcing strategy and assist in evaluating suppliers. Benchmarking industry standards and norms can touch upon standardization, production, purchasing practices, and a number of other areas.

Finally, with respect to costs, an industry analysis must address the selling price and the total cost of ownership. An understanding of production inputs and their prices is necessary to construct the selling price. Total cost of ownership is more comprehensive and includes not only the selling price, but all potential costs related to the good or service before, during, and after the transaction.

While an analysis of the industry in its current state is useful, the factors are not static. Looking only at the current situation leaves the enterprise vulnerable to future supply disruptions, cost increases, and other hazards. It also limits the ability of the enterprise to take advantage of upcoming opportunities. Analysis of historical trends, cycles, and forecasts allows the commodity team to identify and address risks as well as opportunities.

## Identify Potential Suppliers

The next step in market research is to identify and make a list of suppliers of the goods and/or services needed (pp. 47–51).[3] If viable substitute products are available, suppliers of these products should be included on the list of potential suppliers.

Potential suppliers can include current suppliers, former suppliers, and new suppliers.[4] Current and former suppliers are clear candidates, with whom the buyer has previous experi-

---

[3] This process is described for an industry with a number of suppliers, but some industries may have limited competition.

[4] There may be some cases in which all existing suppliers for a product do not meet the needs of the buyer. In these cases, the enterprise may work with a supplier to develop the capabilities to meet the enterprise's needs. Alternatively, the enterprise may also develop a new supplier—perhaps from suppliers producing similar goods or using similar technologies. Such supplier development activities can be costly in terms of effort and resources and so are dependent on the costs and benefits.

ence. New suppliers have not previously contracted with the enterprise; these suppliers may be new entrants, operate in different locations, or offer functional substitutes.

The key to supplier identification is to find and develop good sources of information about suppliers. Some useful resources are an internal supplier database (or other internal forms of supplier records), supplier Web sites and materials such as annual reports and catalogs, personnel within the enterprise and at the supplier, industry sources, trade organizations, journals, and phone directories.

## Evaluate Potential Suppliers

Potential suppliers must be evaluated to determine their suitability. Supplier evaluation is an expensive and resource-intensive process that should be tailored to the importance of the purchase (pp. 53–64). The initial stages of the evaluation process (described below) may be sufficient for noncritical purchases. Supplier evaluation is also an iterative process that eliminates unsuitable suppliers at each stage. Only qualified suppliers advance to more resource-intensive stages of the market research process. The process proceeds as follows:

First, collect basic data on potential suppliers. This preliminary analysis should include a brief evaluation of the following elements: management, finances, references, size, trends, future plans, and other relevant issues (e.g., quality certification). Based on the results, eliminate unqualified suppliers.

Second, conduct a financial evaluation of suppliers. Financial stability is critical because it ensures that the supplier can meet delivery requirements, respond to changes, and meet other demands such as sustained support of the product. Some sample indicators of a supplier's financial health are liquidity measures, funds management ratios, profitability measures, and measures of long-term strength. Eliminate financially unstable suppliers.

Third, analyze the supplier's performance, costs, and capabilities, as follows. Eliminate suppliers who do not meet the necessary requirements:

- Evaluate performance data. Use past performance data for suppliers currently or formerly in the supply base. Use third-party data, supplier data, and supplier "scorecards" for new or potential suppliers.
- Compare the selling price and the total cost of ownership across suppliers.
- Analyze capabilities relevant to the particular good or service required. The most common capabilities assessed are quality, delivery, capacity, and cost. Other capabilities (e.g., technology) should be assessed if they are relevant to the purchase.

Finally, for critical purchases, conduct evaluation conferences between management of the enterprise and each of the remaining suppliers if such meetings would be helpful to the enterprise in making a final selection of the appropriate supplier(s).

## Manage Suppliers

Much of the market research literature focuses on information gathering for source selection (as well as negotiations), but market research does not end when suppliers are selected and the contracts are signed (pp. 65–68). Commercial enterprises use market research to monitor suppliers and changes in markets, ensure that current suppliers remain their best option by tracking performance and other factors, and recognize supplier development needs for current and potential suppliers.

## Where to Look for Relevant Market Research Information

This monograph lists numerous resources for obtaining information for market research. For example, enterprises should have information about their own goals, capabilities, requirements, and sourcing strategies and should have compiled information in their supplier databases on all suppliers who currently or formerly have contracted with the enterprise. External sources—including supplier Web sites and third-party industry observers—can provide a variety of information about the industry in general and about specific suppliers. The commodity teams may also need to collect some data directly from suppliers through requests for information and site visits (i.e., primary data collection).

## Next Steps for the Air Force

The Air Force has made progress toward the implementation of purchasing and supply chain management and market research, including training at Defense Acquisition University and Acquisition Centers of Excellence (such as Warner Robins Air Logistics Center) and provision of online resources. But the implementation of the market research process outlined in this monograph requires additional support from the Air Force. The overriding lessons from the literature and interviews with commercial enterprises are relevant to ensuring the Air Force's success: (1) improve data availability, quality, and utilization; (2) provide training for commodity teams; and (3) ensure the support of top management and buy in among personnel (pp. 69–71).

# Acknowledgments

We wish to thank the purchasing professionals at the commercial firms who took time to meet with us and teach us about their approaches to market research. Assurances of anonymity prevent us from identifying them here, but this research would not have been possible without their help.

We thank Grover Dunn (AF/A4I) for his help in shaping this research to ensure that it addressed the correct issues and concerns. We also thank Air Force procurement personnel for assistance in understanding current market research practices within the Air Force.

We are grateful to our RAND colleagues Mary Chenoweth, Jeremy Arkes, and Laura Baldwin for their insights. Special thanks to David Burt and Susan Gates for their thorough and thoughtful reviews of an earlier draft.

# Abbreviations

| | |
|---|---|
| AF/A4I | U.S. Air Force Deputy Chief of Staff for Logistics, Installations, and Mission Support, Directorate of Transformation |
| CBIS | Contracting Business Intelligence System |
| D&B | Dun & Bradstreet |
| DAU | Defense Acquisition University |
| ISM | Institute for Supply Management |
| JIT | just in time |
| OEM | original equipment manufacturer |
| PAF | Project AIR FORCE |
| PSCM | purchasing and supply chain management |
| RMA | Risk Management Association (formerly Robert Morris Associates) |
| TCO | total cost of ownership |
| TQM | total quality management |
| ZBP | zero base pricing |

# CHAPTER ONE

# Introduction

In a changing security environment that calls for the United States to be ready to respond quickly to a variety of international threats and domestic emergencies, the U.S. Air Force must procure the necessary goods and services efficiently and cost-effectively. The Air Force plans to improve procurement through the implementation of purchasing and supply chain management (PSCM) practices. Among its goals are increasing aircraft availability (i.e., the number of Air Force aircraft that are maintained and ready to fly at any time) by 20 percent over the next five years while reducing costs by 10 percent.[1]

The dual Air Force goals—improved performance and reduced costs—are similar to those of most commercial enterprises. PSCM practices have been successful in achieving similar goals in the commercial sector. The Air Force is taking an important step to emulate the success of commercial enterprises by establishing "commodity councils" to develop proactive, enterprise-wide strategies for purchasing key Air Force goods and services. Commodity councils (or teams) are cross-functional teams of Air Force personnel in charge of developing and implementing sourcing strategies for key groups of like goods and/or services commonly defined as "commodity groups." This approach is intended to replace the functionally oriented approach in which consumers, commodity specialists, and procurement professionals work in isolation from each other and execute specific purchases independently rather than taking into account demands that apply across the Air Force. Each council must understand the needs of the enterprise—in this case, the Air Force—as they relate to its commodity group, strategically manage the supply base, standardize procurement policies and practices across the enterprise, and leverage purchasing volume. Benefits of the commodity council approach should include improved performance in terms of delivery, quality, and costs.

To operate effectively, the commodity teams must build upon specialized knowledge of industries developed from high-quality market research specific to their needs. The research and analysis intrinsic to this process extend beyond the traditional purchasing activities of Air Force procurement personnel. As a result, the Air Force requested assistance from the RAND Corporation to help the commodity teams approach the market research task.

---

[1] These goals are from the Fiscal Year Defense Plan (fiscal year 11) U.S. Air Force Deputy Chief of Staff for Logistics, Installations, and Mission Support (AF/A4/7) goals (U.S. Air Force, 2005). "Stretch" goals for PSCM are a 20 percent increase in aircraft availability with a 20 percent decrease in costs.

## Market Research

> Market analysis is the single most powerful tool in the supply leader's portfolio of skills. It becomes the compass to help navigate a continually changing business jungle.
>
> —*Riggs and Robbins, 1998, p. 66*

### What Is Market Research?

Market research is a process for gathering and analyzing data on industries, markets,[2] and suppliers for the purpose of aligning the needs of an enterprise with the right suppliers on key factors such as quality, delivery, cost, and other key performance indicators. Market research is essential to the identification, evaluation, selection, and maintenance of an optimal supply base. Market research begins with a big picture analysis of the industry pertinent to the good or service, then drills down to identify the pool of potential suppliers, and finally evaluates individual suppliers relative to each other and the industry. Market research should also be ongoing—in that it continues beyond supplier selection to supplier management and development.

### Benefits of Market Research

To the extent that an enterprise can reduce purchasing costs and improve performance, it increases profit and enhances the ability of the enterprise to meet its strategic goals. These goals can include improvements in customer service, quality, and competitiveness, as well as reductions in supply risks. The Air Force may not have an interest in profits per se, but cost savings and performance improvements further its goals of increased aircraft availability at reduced costs. One commercial enterprise we interviewed for this study shared its experiences with implementation of improved PSCM practices. The enterprise had initially projected savings of over $100 million, but actual savings were twice the projected amount. These cost savings represented a significant share of the amount the enterprise spent on purchasing. The literature cites savings of similar magnitude from purchasing and supply initiatives (Avery, 2001). At the same time, this enterprise also experienced substantial improvements in the quality and delivery of purchased goods and services.

Market research is integral to achieving these improvements because it provides the data and analyses to support decisionmaking. But market research is not a stand-alone task; it must be aligned with the enterprise's overall competitive and sourcing strategies. In the ideal situation, the objectives of the enterprise and its supply strategy inform and shape each other. Sourcing strategies are seen as an asset in achieving the enterprise's overall objectives. For example, an enterprise whose competitive strategy is to be the low-cost provider requires a price-sensitive sourcing strategy: It must acquire its production inputs at a low price to ensure that its production costs remain consistent with its target selling price. On the other hand, an enterprise whose competitive strategy is to provide the highest-quality end product may be less

---

[2]    Although the *industry* and *market* are not synonymous, we will henceforth use the term *industry* to avoid confusion with the market research terminology. The issue is explained further in Chapter Three.

price sensitive; its suppliers must be able to provide high-quality inputs that support the enterprise in producing a high-quality end product. For this enterprise, its sourcing strategy ensures that costs are contained without compromising the target quality of the end product.

Market research supports decisionmaking for both the development and the implementation of sourcing strategies. But market research not only takes place when a purchase is required, it also must be a continuous process to ensure that up-to-date knowledge and analyses are available to create and maintain the appropriate supply base.[3] Nor is there a "one-size-fits-all" approach. The intensity of market research required to support a purchase depends in part on the purchase itself. The more intensive elements of market research may be reserved for strategic—high-risk and high-value—purchases.

## Where to Look for Relevant Market Research Information

There are numerous resources for obtaining information for market research. Enterprises should have information about their own goals and purchasing strategies and should have compiled information in their supplier databases on all suppliers that currently or formerly have contracted with the enterprise. External sources—including supplier Web sites and third-party industry observers—can provide a variety of information about the industry in general and about specific suppliers. Finally, some primary data collection may be necessary for strategic purchases. While some primary data collection can be accomplished remotely via requests for information, other information is best collected through site visits. In each chapter of this monograph, we point the reader to sources of data and information relevant to the research question at hand. Appendixes C and D provide listings of specific Internet sources for industry and supplier information.

## Current Air Force Market Research

The Air Force has made progress toward adopting market research techniques, especially through training at the Defense Acquisition University and Warner Robins Air Logistics Center and through the availability of online resources. Warner Robins has been a driving force for market research training and implementation and the center also supports Air Force commodity councils. Warner Robins offers a one-time two-hour workshop to provide just-in-time (JIT) training for existing personnel who are tasked with procurement and general training for new personnel. Additionally, the Air Force has made resources available online. For example, two publications from the U.S. Department of Defense (1996 and 1997) outline the basic principles of market research, emphasize the importance of market research at each stage of the acquisition process, and highlight the data requirements to support market research.

---

[3]   The Air Force, in its approach to market research, differentiates these two activities. *Market surveillance* includes market research activities required to ensure that relevant personnel remain aware of changes in the market, products, and industry. *Market investigation* is the Air Force's terminology for market research associated with a particular purchase.

The complex analyses inherent in market research go beyond traditional Air Force procurement activities. Commodity teams need to understand what to analyze, how to analyze it, and how to obtain and develop the data required for the analyses. The status of Air Force market research is described in Chapter Seven of this monograph, along with suggestions for integrating current Air Force efforts with the recommendations of this monograph.

## Approach

RAND focused on identifying the best commercial practices for market research. Our approach included a review of the PSCM literature and interviews with commercial enterprises identified as best in class with respect to their procurement practices.

### Literature Review

Best practices and recent advances with respect to market research were drawn from a review of the literature, including textbooks and periodicals. The composite market research process described in this monograph is a compilation of elements drawn and adapted from these sources. The composite process relies heavily on textbooks—specifically, Porter, 1980; Burt, Dobler, and Starling, 2003; Leenders et al., 2001; Leenders and Blenkhorn, 1988; Monczka, Trent, and Handfield, 2001; and Raedels, 2000.[4] Articles from publications such as *Purchasing* were used to supplement these sources.

Most of the textbooks reviewed for this document focused primarily on purchasing. However, to provide background material for the reader who is relatively new to the subject of analyzing the competitiveness of industries, we summarize Porter, 1980. The first section of Chapter Three contains a detailed summary of Porter's analysis of market forces. We use Porter's framework as a structure to identify key issues for analysis and detail how these issues affect sourcing. Readers who are familiar with Porter's work may skip this section.

### Interviews with Successful Commercial Enterprises

During the review of the literature, we identified several leading commercial enterprises from which to solicit interviews. The purpose of the interviews was to draw on the experiences of leading commercial enterprises to supplement the processes and guidance available in the literature. The literature does not single out enterprises for their performance in market research techniques; rather, the literature identifies enterprises that have developed best practices for purchasing. Because successful purchasing should build upon effective market research, RAND selected enterprises based on their purchasing reputations. Assurances of anonymity prevent us from identifying the enterprises here, but these enterprises have been singled out in the literature as exemplars and/or have received recognition in their industries and/or within the procurement community. We interviewed over a dozen purchasing executives and managers, including directors of strategic sourcing at four U.S. commercial enterprises. These enterprises

---

[4]   Readers interested in additional detail are referred to these sources.

have varied perspectives on market research based on their industries and on their progress in implementing PSCM initiatives.

Selection of enterprises was also based on their relevance to the Air Force. Efforts were made to identify leading commercial enterprises that do business with industries, markets, and suppliers similar to those the Air Force encounters. The enterprises interviewed were primarily in the aerospace, machinery manufacturing, and automotive manufacturing industries. To conduct the interviews, RAND staff traveled to the enterprise locations to meet in person with top personnel involved in purchasing and supply management. A copy of the interview protocol used in these interviews is included in Appendix A.

It would have been useful to conduct additional interviews. However, a number of commercial enterprises contacted for this study were unable to participate. Some commercial enterprises identified as leading cited "fatigue." These enterprises have been inundated with similar requests for interviews, often from government agencies. Also, with the improvement in the economy, personnel at many of these enterprises were busy ramping up operations. Another reason cited for refusal to participate included changes in management personnel, which focused resources on transitional activities.

## About This Monograph

### Key Terms and Concepts

Many readers will understand the terms and concepts that we use in this discussion of market research. However, many of the terms and concepts have applications and meanings that are different or broader in other contexts than they are intended to be here. Therefore, we provide some basic definitions in Table 1.1 to ensure consistent understanding by all readers.

### Organization of This Monograph

This monograph is organized around the composite process for conducting market research. It begins with background information, proceeds through some of the how-to steps for conducting market research, and ends with recommendations for next steps. In each chapter, we provide background information and highlight lessons learned from both our literature review and from our interviews with personnel at leading commercial enterprises. Chapter by chapter, the monograph is organized as follows:

- Chapter Two emphasizes the importance of certain preliminary steps that should be completed before the crux of market research begins. The commodity team must be aware of the enterprise's strategic goals, competencies, and requirements as they relate to the good or service, understand the enterprise's spend, and develop a tailored sourcing strategy. These factors assist the commodity team in allocating resources for market research and directing market research efforts.

**Table 1.1**
**Glossary**

| Term | Definition |
| --- | --- |
| Benchmark | To identify and/or measure a reference point for comparison |
| Capabilities | The ability of an enterprise to undertake certain activities such as engineering, quality control, etc. Capabilities are not to be confused with capacity |
| Capacity | An enterprise's potential production volume |
| Commodity council (or commodity team) | Teams of cross-functional personnel responsible for developing and implementing enterprise-wide proactive, tailored supply strategies for purchasing specific groups of goods and services |
| Enterprise | Commercial firms, nonprofit organizations, or government organizations such as the Air Force. In this text, we use this term to refer specifically to the buyer of a good or service |
| Inputs | Raw materials, labor, and other factors used to produce a good or service |
| Market research | The process of gathering and analyzing data on industries, markets, and suppliers of goods and services for the purpose of aligning the needs of an enterprise with the right suppliers on key factors such as costs, delivery, and quality |
| Should-cost estimate | A calculation of the selling price of a good or service |
| Sourcing strategy | The approach developed by the commodity council to procure a good or service (or a group of goods or services). The sourcing strategy relates to the buying policy, the number of suppliers, the type of source, and the supplier relationship (Raedels, 2000) |
| Spend | The enterprise's total expenditures on goods and services |
| Spend analysis | The analysis of expenditures by commodity group, individual commodity, supplier, and other relevant characteristics |
| Total cost of ownership | All of the costs associated with the purchase of the good or service—including costs incurred before, during, and after the transaction |

- Chapter Three describes the first step in market research—analyzing the industry related to the good or service. The focus of the chapter is on how competition, industry standards and norms, and cost analyses affect sourcing. This chapter also discusses the importance of analyzing trends, cycles, and forecasts to identify and address both risks and opportunities. An understanding of the industry can drive later steps in market research, including supplier identification, evaluation, and management.
- Chapter Four describes the second step in market research: identifying potential suppliers of relevant goods and services. This chapter focuses on the sources used for supplier identification and highlights their strengths and weaknesses.
- Chapter Five describes the third step in market research: evaluating the potential suppliers identified in the previous step. The suppliers must be evaluated relative to each other and to the industry as a whole on key characteristics and performance indicators.
- Chapter Six notes that market research does not end with the evaluation and selection of the best suppliers. The enterprise must continually manage and develop the supply base.

- Chapter Seven discusses the current state of market research in the Air Force, highlights some implementation issues encountered by commercial enterprises, and makes recommendations for the Air Force on how to support market research activities.

The appendixes provide additional resources or background information too lengthy or detailed to be included within the text of this monograph, such as summaries, sample resource lists, and sample templates. They are organized as follows:

- Appendix A contains the interview protocol that RAND developed for this project and used when interviewing purchasing personnel from commercial enterprises.
- Appendix B provides additional detail on the elements of the sourcing strategy, including definitions of elements.
- Appendix C lists some Internet sites that may be helpful to practitioners looking for market research information. For example, it lists Web addresses for industry and trade associations, government Web sites, and purchasing organizations.
- Appendix D lists Internet sites that may be helpful to practitioners looking for specific financial data on industries and suppliers, and discusses the interpretation of financial ratios. For example, the Dun & Bradstreet (known as D&B) Web site provides short reports on millions of companies worldwide and provides subscribers with credit reports on organizations.
- Appendix E offers sample tools that are provided in the market research literature. These include questionnaires for evaluating supplier quality, organization, and management; an evaluation survey to use during visits to plant facilities; and a sample supplier scorecard.

# CHAPTER TWO

# Focus Market Research Resources and Efforts Where They Are Most Needed

Because market research is both expensive and time-consuming and because resources at most enterprises are limited, market research should be focused on the areas that are most vital and beneficial. Not every purchase warrants intensive market research. The enterprise must look inward to determine where its efforts will yield the greatest return. To allocate market research resources and effort properly, the commodity team must understand the enterprise's strategic goals, competencies, requirements as they relate to the good or service, spend, and sourcing strategy.

## Collect the Facts About the Enterprise

### Understand Strategic Goals, Competencies, and Requirements

The commodity team's market research efforts must be consistent with the enterprise's strategic goals, competencies, and requirements, so a preliminary step is to gather information on these subjects. Information should be available from mission statements for the enterprise or unit, internal documents such as design specifications, and personnel (e.g., engineers).

Strategic goals indicate what the enterprise is trying to accomplish. A commercial enterprise may be focused on increasing profit or market share. For the Air Force, recent goals include increasing aircraft availability at reduced costs. Such goals inform the sourcing strategy and direct market research efforts.

Enterprises should also consider core competencies when deciding which goods and services should be sourced rather than produced or provided in-house. The decision is based on the ability of the enterprise to produce a competitive good or service. This is a function of technological capabilities, labor skills, availability of inputs and facilities, and access to any necessary proprietary information. It is also a function of effectiveness. The enterprise may be able to produce the product, but can its production compete with other suppliers on key performance indicators including cost, quality, and delivery? The Air Force may also consider these issues. For example, does the Air Force have the personnel, training, and know-how to provide aftermarket support for aircraft engines?[1] Can it do so in a competitive way? If the Air

---

[1]  The Air Force is also subject to regulations such as the 50-50 law for maintenance.

Force cannot, then sourcing is preferred to internal provision (subject to strategic concerns). Appendix B provides additional detail on the make-or-buy decision.

Requirements indicate what the enterprise needs. What goods and services are needed? What specifications and level of performance are necessary to achieve the enterprise's goals?

## Analyze Spending

A spend analysis explores the enterprise's spending overall and analyzes expenditures by commodity, supplier, and other relevant categories. In essence, this is internal research on the enterprise itself. This analysis is useful not only for allocating market research resources, but also to support the market research process. Throughout this monograph, it should be clear that market research and the decisionmaking it supports rely on an understanding of enterprise spend.

Spend analysis identifies which products and suppliers comprise a significant portion of expenditures. The enterprise must be able to answer the following basic questions about its current expenditures:

- What is the enterprise's current total spend?
- What percentage of spend is purchased goods and services (versus internal labor, etc.)?
- What percentage of spend is goods versus services?
- What is the distribution of spend by commodity group?
- What is the distribution of spend by commodity code for strategic purchases?
- What is the distribution of spend across suppliers?
- What is the source of internal demand (i.e., users)?

To address these questions, the enterprise must record and categorize expenditures in terms of the item purchased (e.g., commodity code or commodity group), the quantity, the supplier, the price, the user, and the frequency of purchase. Such detailed data require that the enterprise have in place or implement an expenditure tracking system that records each of these elements. This is not a simple task. Enterprises have spent millions of dollars and substantial personnel hours implementing software systems to track expenditures accurately and comprehensively. While implementing expenditure tracking, commercial enterprises sometimes rely on interim databases and information from their suppliers (subject to audit verification). The Air Force has existing data sources—such as the Contracting Business Intelligence System (CBIS)—that are useful starting points for spend analyses.

## Develop (or Update) the Sourcing Strategy[2]

Each commodity team is tasked with developing a proactive and tailored supply strategy for the goods and services in its commodity group. A sourcing strategy is a work in progress—especially in the initial stages of setting up a commodity council. The strategy should rely on the analysis of internal factors described above as well as the market research described in the following chapters. But before beginning the market research process, the commodity team must

---

[2]  This section draws from Raedels, 2000, and Burt, Dobler, and Starling, 2003.

> **Interview Lessons: Tracking Spend Comprehensively**
>
> The enterprises interviewed for this study used a variety of software to record spend. Personnel cautioned, however, that having the software is not enough. The data must be comprehensive and accurate. The implementation and operation must ensure that the software tracks all spending. Backdoor* and off-contract purchases are prohibited. One enterprise noted that it took action against personnel who engaged in backdoor purchasing. Many commercial enterprises were not initially equipped to undertake such detailed tracking and analysis. One enterprise delayed the PSCM implementation process for a year to ensure that the software had collected sufficient data for analysis.
>
> *Backdoor or maverick spend are purchases that circumvent the procurement process.

have an understanding of the basic elements of a sourcing strategy and how the information collected on the enterprise, industry, and suppliers shapes the development of that strategy.

There are four basic elements of a sourcing strategy: the buying policy, the number of sources, the type of source, and the supplier relationship. How those components are managed depends, in part, on the market research outlined in this monograph. We briefly discuss some of the central issues here. Additional detail is provided in Appendix B, which contains definitions summarized from Raedels, 2000, and Burt, Dobler, and Starling, 2003. Appendix B also provides some context for how market research, in turn, affects the development of the sourcing strategy.

The *buying policy* relates to the type of "buys" or purchases to be made: subsistence, forward, volume purchase agreements; life-of-product supply; consignment; or end-of-life buys.[3] This choice should be based on the criticality and strategic nature of the buy, keeping in mind that the decision affects the enterprise's leverage with suppliers, production schedules, and inventory costs. The buying policy must ensure that production schedules are not compromised by ensuring supply while minimizing inventory costs. The policy should also leverage purchasing volume throughout the enterprise.[4] Market research should identify industry norms on the type of buy.

The choice of buying policy should be determined by the best interest of the enterprise though it may be influenced by industry norms. Is this particular purchase strategic and critical to the production process? Is it purchased frequently? If so, then reactive purchasing types (such as subsistence buys) will be inappropriate because they fail to proactively manage supply. Instead, the enterprise should consider more proactive and strategic options such as volume purchase agreements. Subsistence buys are useful for one-time unexpected purchases. Commercial

---

[3] For additional detail and definitions, see Appendix B. We exclude speculative buys from the list because of its limited relevance to the Air Force.

[4] In some cases, commercial enterprises negotiate contracts that include an option for their own suppliers to purchase on the same terms (e.g., same price) in order to increase their own purchasing leverage and to secure lower prices for their suppliers and thereby reduce their own costs.

enterprises also use consignment arrangements (such as vendor-managed inventory) to keep stock on hand while minimizing inventory and managing the timing of expenditures for particular types of purchases (e.g., commodities). More specific buying policies, such as end-of-life buys and life-of-product supply, may be appropriate for low-demand or obsolete goods that are an important component for an end product when ongoing customer support is essential.

---

**Interview Lessons: Proactive Buying Policies**

Proactive buying policies are useful tools for management of supply, but they present their own issues. For example, one concern with *volume purchase agreements* is the uncertainty of future demand. To address this, some enterprises did not specify the exact quantities to be purchased over the contract term (e.g., five years). Rather, they provided the suppliers with a best estimate of demand based on their internal analyses and negotiated price-volume discounts based on these estimates. However, they did not commit to particular purchase quantities. Likewise, it is tempting to rely on lean JIT systems to minimize inventory costs and ensure a flow of inputs to production processes. However, implementing lean systems is difficult. Enterprises that have successfully incorporated lean systems caution that it is not possible to do so without including suppliers in the lean process. Training, however, can be expensive and often out of the reach of smaller suppliers. In response, some enterprises offered lean training to their key suppliers.

---

**Interview Lessons: Ensuring Supply of Obsolete and Low-Demand Goods**

Goods whose production is being discontinued or for which the enterprise has only limited demand can be difficult to source effectively. Market research is critical to making an informed decision regarding the best approach to addressing these purchases.

Some enterprises we interviewed engaged in *end-of-life buys* for a limited number of obsolete goods. One enterprise indicated that end-of-life buys assisted in the commitment to support customers after purchase. The decision is based on the competitive strategy of the enterprise (e.g., with respect to customer support and satisfaction), cost concerns such as price and inventory costs, anticipated demand, and the availability of alternative sources—issues that are made clear in market research. But it may not be cost-effective to stock all obsolete goods. An enterprise might forgo an end-of-life buy if (1) inventory costs are too high, (2) surplus suppliers carry these items even after production has ceased, and (3) the enterprise has the capacity to reverse engineer the good in-house.

Enterprises whose competitive strategy was customer service sometimes engaged in *life-of-product* contracts for low-demand goods. These contracts ensured that there would be a supplier for the critical parts for as long as the enterprise had committed to support its end user. The decision to adopt a life-of-product contract followed directly from the enterprise's competitive strategy. However, cost considerations for low-demand items mitigate the use of these contracts. For cases in which the enterprise had the capability (and capacity) and did own the design for the part, it was sometimes more cost-effective for the enterprise to manufacture its own parts.

> **Interview Lessons: The Commodity Team as the One Face to the Supplier**
>
> A single contract (or a minimal number of contracts) with each supplier improves the enterprise's ability to leverage spend while minimizing the administration and transaction costs. Managing multiple contracts with each supplier is a key cost driver because enterprises generally spend 70 to 80 percent of spend with their top suppliers. One enterprise stressed that the use of a single "master" contract was important in limiting the supplier's ability to "divide and conquer." In traditional tactical purchasing, each unit or site of the enterprise might deal independently with the same supplier. Or alternatively, different commodities might be purchased separately from the same supplier. When the enterprises analyzed their contract relationships, they found that units within the enterprise often paid substantially different prices to the same supplier for the same product. To counteract this phenomenon, the enterprises recommended "one face" to the supplier and a single contract. Personnel on the commodity team are typically the one face to the supplier. The lead contact was the person from the team who represented the unit with the largest share of that supplier's business.

The *number of sources* is a critical element of the sourcing strategy. There are three main categories for this element of the sourcing plan: sole source, single source, and multiple source. Sole source refers to situations in which there is only one supplier available. Single source refers to the use of only one supplier even though other suppliers are available. Multiple source refers to the use of more than one supplier. Commercial enterprises have recently engaged in substantial supply base rationalization in an attempt to leverage purchasing power and reduce total costs. This process focuses on achieving the right mix of suppliers for each commodity and often results in reducing the number of suppliers utilized.

In keeping with supply base rationalization, some commercial enterprises will use only the minimum number of suppliers necessary to meet the buyer's demand. In some cases, this will be a single supplier while in other cases multiple suppliers are necessary. Using a single or the minimum number of suppliers necessary is a simple way to reduce transaction costs and leverage purchasing power. But there are risks in making the supply chain too lean. To take advantage of the benefits of fewer suppliers while minimizing the risk of supply disruptions, some commercial enterprises have undertaken an "$n + 1$" approach. Commodity teams calculate $n$ as the minimum number of suppliers necessary to satisfy demand, but engage $n + 1$ suppliers to ensure that additional supply is available within the supply base.

In selecting the appropriate number of suppliers, commercial enterprises consider the share of the supplier's capacity dedicated to the buyer's demand. The concern is that higher shares may create undue dependence on the part of the supplier. If a supplier is dependent on a buyer, the buyer may be hesitant or restricted in its ability to switch from a poorly performing supplier (because of the knowledge that it may undermine the supplier's viability). A rule of thumb is that the buyer's needs should not represent more than 15 to 25 percent of the supplier's capacity (Burt, Dobler, and Starling, 2003).[5] On the other hand, commercial enterprises interviewed also cautioned about being too small a share (e.g., less than 0.5 percent) of the sup-

---

[5]  This is a rule of thumb, but it is subject to the makeup of the particular industry.

plier's capacity, because shares that are too small do not motivate the supplier to be responsive to the buyer. Of course, the importance of a lower bound depends on the type of purchase. For example, it may not be as important for transactional purchases that can be easily and (almost) costlessly switched across suppliers when performance is unsatisfactory.

A final concern in choosing the number of suppliers is the issue of proprietary information. In general, proprietary information should be shared with a limited number of suppliers.

---

**Interview Lessons: Single Sourcing for Low-Demand Items**

One enterprise offered suppliers single source contracts for the life of the product in exchange for each supplier's promise to supply particular parts as long as necessary. Single sourcing can be used for a single low-demand item when market research reveals that the volume is too low relative to supplier size. Alternatively, if demand is still too low to attract suppliers even in a life-of-product contract, enterprises may combine similar low-demand items into one bid (or combine a low-demand item with a similar high-demand item). Commodities may be similar enough in terms of production process, necessary tooling, or raw materials to allow the supplier to capture some efficiencies, economies of scale, or economies of scope.

---

**Interview Lessons: Number of Suppliers and Supply Base Rationalization**

Spend analyses and market research can highlight opportunities for cost savings from a reduced number of suppliers. Enterprises we interviewed had approximately 70 to 80 percent of dollar spend with their top suppliers. The number of suppliers can be a key driver of sourcing cost. The enterprises interviewed for this study had engaged in significant supply base rationalization. Although these enterprises still engaged hundreds of suppliers, the bulk of their spend was concentrated among a very few select suppliers. One enterprise had reduced its supply base to one-third of its original size over the course of five years. The remaining suppliers were carefully chosen from among the original supply base. As a result, there was greatly increased loyalty, better pricing, and little remaining turnover in the supply base.

---

The *type of source* involves the type of supplier to be used in the sourcing process. Elements of this decision include the size, location, geographic coverage, and diversity status of the supplier.

The choice of supplier size depends on the size of the purchase. The buyer's share of supplier capacity should be large enough to engender supplier responsiveness, but not large enough to create supplier dependence. As noted above, the buyer should not represent more than 15 to 25 percent of a supplier's production (Burt, Dobler, and Starling, 2003) or less than 0.5 percent. As noted earlier, the importance of a lower bound depends on the type of purchase and the ease and cost of switching suppliers.

Geographic location can be an issue for certain types of buys. For example, the criticality of some purchases or the costs of shipping may argue for a local supplier or for a national supplier with local facilities. National suppliers may be preferred when goods or services are required at multiple facilities to ensure a similar product and to minimize the transaction costs of searching for a supplier for each location. On the other hand, local providers may be preferred when a good or service is procured for a single site. Similar concerns affect the decision to source domestically versus internationally, although international buys involve additional concerns relating to cultural and legal differences, customs, tariffs, quotas, exchange rates, and communication. Issues involving proprietary information are also a concern when choosing the type of source. For example, limiting the number of suppliers with access to sensitive information may influence the decision to select a single national supplier rather than a local supplier for each site (and the decision to use a domestic rather than an international supplier).

Additionally, commercial enterprises may have mandatory or voluntary socioeconomic goals that direct the use of small, minority-owned, women-owned, service-disabled veteran-owned, or local suppliers. Some commercial enterprises direct their supplier diversity efforts to the 20 percent of spend not accounted for by their key suppliers. Others may find that diversity suppliers (e.g., a small business) offer new technological innovations in critical components that can benefit the enterprise.

**Interview Lessons: Supporting Diversity Suppliers**

Unlike government agencies, commercial enterprises may not have a federal mandate to support small, disadvantaged, service-disabled veteran-owned, minority-owned, and women-owned businesses. However, some enterprises had instituted their own socioeconomic goals to promote these businesses. The enterprises offered assistance to these businesses in the form of mentoring and training to assist them in the request-for-proposal process. However, the enterprises stressed that these suppliers were required to be competitive.

The final component is the type of *supplier relationship*. Many commercial enterprises are moving from arms-length to deeper supplier relationships. But even these enterprises do not develop deep supplier relationships with all suppliers. Rather, they stratify their supply base based on the criticality of the purchase. Strategic supplier relationships, such as supplier alliances, are reserved for critical purchases. Nonstrategic items, such as generic commodities available from many suppliers, continue to be purchased in a contractual manner. It is important to note, however, that this does not preclude the use of longer-term consolidated contracts or price-volume agreements that allow the enterprise to leverage its purchasing power and reduce transaction costs. Table B.2 (from Tang, 1999) in Appendix B provides a matrix linking supplier relationship to the characteristics of the purchase.

---

**Interview Lessons: Strategic Arrangements**

Because the enterprises had recently engaged in supply base rationalization, the remaining key suppliers were considered long-term strategic partners. The enterprises were exploring methods for aligning their operations more closely with suppliers via integrated supply chain management. The process requires that the enterprise and the supplier share additional information. Enterprises were moving toward sharing information on demand and other factors so that suppliers could become more integrated with the enterprise. Developing trust was an important element of this process.

---

## Allocate Market Research Resources and Efforts to Maximize Rewards and Minimize Risks

Market research efforts should be focused where they will generate the greatest benefit to the enterprise. Simply collecting the information is not sufficient. Analysis of the data is vital to making informed decisions about allocating market research efforts. Pareto analysis and portfolio analysis are among the most common tools for analyzing and allocating scarce resources. Pareto analysis offers a simple method for characterizing importance based on expenditures, while portfolio analysis allows more factors to be considered in the analyses and so produces a more nuanced evaluation.

Pareto analysis, also known as ABC analysis, groups commodities into categories based on spend and volume. Three categories, "A," "B," and "C," are commonly used. Pareto analysis is useful in setting priorities and the level of effort for each purchase. Table 2.1 demonstrates the general insight of Pareto analysis. A small number of commodities form a significant part of spend. Sourcing efforts should be focused on these high-value goods and services. Items in Group A include only 10 to 20 percent of purchases but account for 70 to 80 percent of total spend. This statement is consistent with findings from commercial enterprises. These items are high-value because they account for so much of the enterprise's expenditures. As a result, they require more-detailed market research and receive the most attention in the sourcing strategy. Approximately 30 to 50 percent of goods and services fall into Group B; this group accounts

**Table 2.1**
**Pareto Analysis**

| Group | Market Research Effort | Percentage of Products | Percentage of Spend |
|-------|------------------------|------------------------|---------------------|
| A | Most attention | 10–20 | 70–80 |
| B | Some attention | 30–50 | 30–50 |
| C | Least attention | 40–70 | 10–20 |

SOURCE: Adapted from Carter, 1999 p. 82.

NOTE: The percentages of spend are intervals and, therefore, do not sum to 100 percent.

for 30 to 50 percent of spend. These items receive some attention in the sourcing strategy and market research, but not as much as Group A. Finally, the remaining 40 to 70 percent of items contained in Group C account for the final 10 to 20 percent of spend. These low-dollar items are generally routine purchases.[6] As such, they require and receive little attention in the market research and sourcing process unless they are bundled together into a much larger purchase.

Pareto analysis also offers insights into other opportunities for improved sourcing behavior, such as reducing the number of suppliers in the supply base and consolidation of contracts. The relationship between spend and the number of suppliers often mimics that between spend and products. Leading commercial enterprises typically concentrate 70 to 80 percent of spend with less than 20 percent of their supply base.[7]

A limitation of the Pareto analysis is that it focuses only on dollars spent and volume. It ignores other factors such as the criticality of an item to production and the risk inherent in limited supply or suppliers. Nor does it account for the fact that purchase costs are only one factor in the total cost of ownership (TCO).

A more flexible approach to analyzing spend is a portfolio analysis, which focuses on vulnerability and value. In essence, this approach quantifies the relative risk and rewards of each good or service and so can be useful when a simple analysis of spending dollars (i.e., Pareto analysis) is insufficient to properly characterize the importance of certain purchases to the enterprise. The factors that determine the importance of market research for any particular good or service are broadly categorized as *value* and *vulnerability* (see, e.g., Monczka, Trent, and Handfield, 2001; Leenders et al., 2001). Each commodity team must conduct its own analyses appropriate for the type of goods and services for which they are responsible. Greater resources are allocated to obtaining items with greater value and vulnerability.

Value can be measured as the dollars expended and financial effects, the strategic importance of the product to the enterprise's production process, importance to customer satisfaction, or the technical complexity of the item being purchased. High-dollar-value, strategically important or technically complex purchases require more-intensive research to minimize the harm of potential supply disruptions. To assess value, the enterprise must look at the distribution of its expenditures, its strategic goals, and how the good or service being purchased affects the enterprise's end product (e.g., in terms of quality).

Vulnerability can be measured by the importance of the good or service, the risk of supply interruptions, limited number of sources of supply and substitutes,[8] or the inability of the enterprise's current supply base to meet the product requirements (e.g., specifications, degree of customization, and technology). Other risk factors include unpredictable demand or usage. Assessment of vulnerability requires a thorough understanding of the enterprise's demand and supply for a good or service.

---

[6]  Routine purchases can consist of low-value purchases of true "commodity" goods and services.

[7]  A recent article indicates that leading commercial enterprises concentrate up to 80 percent of their spend with less than 6 percent of their supply base ("Hacket Report Finds Best Procurement Orgs See Greater ROI," 2005).

[8]  The number of potential suppliers is not strictly an internal factor in that it encompasses some assessment of the market, but it should be noted that this information is used to assess the vulnerability of the enterprise with respect to the product to be purchased.

Figure 2.1 illustrates this approach to directing market research efforts using value and vulnerability. Quadrant I requires the least intensive market research effort because both value and vulnerability are minimal. These products have a low cost and are not critical inputs. Likewise, the existing or potential supply base is capable of fulfilling the requirements. Widely available, low-value, standardized commodities such as fasteners would fall into this category. The purchases in Quadrant II require some market research to ensure that the best suppliers are being used. These products have substantial value in terms of volume and dollars, but often have several sources of supply and low costs associated with switching suppliers, which minimize the risk of supply disruptions. Purchases of jet fuel would fall into this quadrant. Purchases in Quadrant III are risky because they have unique specifications and few sources of supply and substitutes. But the low value indicates that market research should be limited because the costs of intensive market research may outweigh the value of the purchase. Nonstandard parts that require unique modifications or specifications fall into this category. The strategic purchases in Quadrant IV require the most intensive market research. These goods and services may have high dollar value, unique specifications, or are critical to the enterprise's end product. These purchases are also vulnerable because of limited sources of

**Figure 2.1**
**Portfolio Analysis**

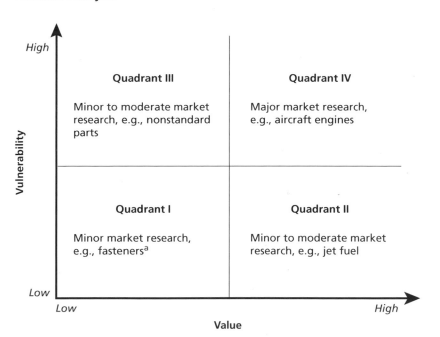

SOURCE: Adapted from Carter, 1999; Monczka, Trent, and Handfield, 2001; and Leenders et al., 2001.

[a] In general, standardized "commodity-type" fasteners require little market research. But there are exceptions; for instance, highly specified (or specially modified) fasteners would require more-intensive effort.

RAND MG473-2.1

supply, lack of substitutes, or high costs to switch suppliers. For the Air Force, aircraft engines represent a strategic product that would require intensive market research.

Both Pareto and portfolio analyses can be useful in focusing market research efforts, but commodity teams must also be aware of any particular issues facing the enterprise. For example, the teams must also address problems with the production cost and quality of an end product if these problems are traced to underperforming suppliers rather than internal processes. Also, in their simplest forms, these analysis approaches focus on only the current situation, which limits opportunities for improvement. Past trends, cycles, and future changes are also vital. Looking back will reveal which goods and services experienced substantial variation in price and demand (or other factors) and where market research into available suppliers and substitutes might limit the enterprise's vulnerability. Projections regarding the future are also important. For example, the implementation of a new production process, which shifts the mix of inputs, will change the needs of the enterprise. Projections of spend on these inputs will highlight a need to downsize contracts for some inputs and to research new sources or relationships for others. Budget forecasts that affect the sourcing strategy are also relevant. The benefit of a forward-looking analysis ensures that the change does not penalize the enterprise in terms of cost, quality, schedule, and other key performance metrics.

## Summary

### Review: What to Do

Before beginning market research, it is important to put the market research in context—to have an understanding of the enterprise (i.e., the U.S. Air Force)—that will help direct market research efforts toward the areas in which limited time and resources provide the greatest benefit. The following list summarizes the suggestions and action steps discussed in this chapter.

1. Understand the enterprise's goals, capabilities, and requirements.
2. Compile and analyze spend data for the relevant commodity groups and their components.
3. Develop (or update) approaches to the four components of the sourcing strategy: buying policy, number of sources, type of source, and supplier relationship.
4. Allocate limited market research resources to areas with the greatest potential benefit to the enterprise.
5. Be aware of particular end-product issues (e.g., quality or lack of profitability) that are traced back to poor performance by suppliers and of how trends, cycles, and future changes affect sourcing.

### Where to Look for Relevant Information

The following sources of information will be helpful in conducting the preliminary analyses described in this chapter:

- internal documents and personnel
  - mission statements
  - relevant personnel (e.g., engineers)
  - relevant documents (e.g., design specifications)
- spend data and budget forecasts (e.g., CBIS)
- sourcing strategy document (if available).

# CHAPTER THREE

# Analyze the Industry

Once the commodity team understands the internal issues discussed in the previous chapter, it can look outward and begin market research specific to a particular good or service. The first step in market research is to develop an understanding of the industry pertinent to the good or service.[1] This industry analysis touches upon factors that affect sourcing: the competitiveness of an industry, industry standards and industry norms, and costs. It is useful to start the market research process with this general overview of the industry and then work toward a more detailed investigation of the factors that are most relevant to the industry. The industry analysis will then also shape the identification, evaluation, and management of suppliers described in later chapters.

First, the commodity team should assess how competitive an industry is and how that competitiveness affects sourcing. For example, if an industry report indicates that the industry is declining (e.g., the market is shrinking), then there should be competition among suppliers for remaining demand. This competition, in turn, should improve sourcing opportunities with respect to cost and other performance indicators. The analysis should then examine more deeply which suppliers are most competitive and viable (in the long term) and why. The analysis may reveal economies of scope—production synergies for suppliers who produce two or more related products—which are essential to lowering supplier costs and to suppliers' long-term financial health. The enterprise may then identify and evaluate suppliers keeping in mind that those who produce multiple products may offer lower prices and may represent less supply risk because they are financially stable.

Second, it is important that an industry analysis "benchmark"—identify and measure—industry standards and norms. Benchmarks are useful rules of thumb that can guide the sourcing strategy and assist in evaluating suppliers. Benchmarking industry standards and norms can touch upon standardization, production, purchasing practices, and a number of other areas.

Finally, with respect to costs, an industry analysis must address the selling price and the TCO. An understanding of production inputs and their prices is necessary to construct the selling price. TCO is more comprehensive and includes not only the selling price but all potential costs related to the good or service before, during, and after the transaction.

---

[1] *Market* and *industry* are not synonymous. A supplier from another industry may offer a substitute product that would be in the "market." However, we will use the term *industry* here to encompass an industry and its substitutes in order to avoid confusion with the market research terminology.

While an analysis of the industry in its current state is useful, the factors addressed in this chapter are not static. Looking at only the current situation leaves the enterprise vulnerable to future supply disruptions, cost increases, and other hazards. It also limits the ability of the enterprise to take advantage of upcoming opportunities. Analysis of historical trends, cycles, and forecasts allows the commodity team to identify and address risks as well as opportunities.

An important element of this process is information. Throughout this chapter, we list sources for market research information. Three types of sources are most common: industry studies by third-party observers, journal publications, and supplier sources. Industry studies are useful because they give a general overview of the industry and often provide benchmark data. In essence, some market research has already been done by trade associations, consulting firms, academic institutions and individuals, government agencies, and other third-party observers. Industry studies vary in length, depth, and focus and may include full-length books by academics and shorter studies by consulting firms.[2] There are trade-offs, however: For example, these more in-depth resources are less timely and less frequently produced than shorter journal articles. The focus of these resources may also be different. These studies may focus on aggregate trends (e.g., prices and costs); market concentration and key players in an industry; or the underlying mechanisms for change, such as key cost drivers, technology, seasonality and cyclicality, and potential infringement by substitute products. Journal articles from trade and purchasing organizations may provide timelier information or recent developments within the industry. Additional information may be obtained from suppliers through Web sites, annual reports, and other sources. Supplier sources, however, generally provide less of an overview and may be more useful to clarify and dig deeper into issues identified in the overview. Recently, market intelligence research firms have made information on industries and suppliers available, usually at a cost.

## Assess How Competitive the Industry Is and How That Affects Sourcing

Sourcing is affected by the level of competition within an industry. "Perfect" competition ensures that suppliers are "price takers" (i.e., a single supplier cannot unduly influence the price of a product), generally because there are numerous suppliers producing the same good or service. Suppliers cannot deviate too far in terms of their product or price. In such a market, a buyer may purchase the good or service easily with little market research because there is little or no price variation, differences in the product, penalties or costs associated with switching from one supplier to another, or risk of running low on supply. However, when competition is not perfect, an enterprise can benefit from conducting market research, especially for goods and services that represent high value or high risk to the enterprise.

How can the commodity team determine when an industry is competitive? Michael E. Porter, 1980, develops a framework for analyzing the competitiveness of an industry. The

---

[2]   Appendix C provides specific resources.

framework identifies five forces that can restrict or enhance competition in an industry: (1) entry barriers, (2) threat of substitutes, (3) bargaining power of suppliers, (4) rivalry among existing suppliers, and (5) bargaining power of buyers (see Figure 3.1).

In this section, we use Porter's framework to identify and summarize the key issues relating to the five forces that determine the competitiveness of an industry. Commodity teams must be aware of these factors and key issues when analyzing the industry and assess how they might affect the enterprise's sourcing strategy. Tables 3.1 through 3.5 summarize the five forces and key issues, providing examples and identifying resources from which commodity teams can obtain more information about the relevance of each factor (drawn from Porter, 1980; Cox et al., 2002). While the framework follows Porter's analysis of industry competition, the focus of its application in this chapter is not an investigation of competitiveness for its own sake, but rather an understanding of how competition shapes sourcing decisions. More knowledgeable readers may choose to skim these background subsections.

A detailed analysis of all of the factors and issues described in this section would be costly and time intensive. It should be clear that not all factors and issues are relevant to every industry. Rather, these tables identify issues that commodity teams should keep in mind when learning about an industry so that they can identify issues to pursue further. Starting with a broad

**Figure 3.1**
**Factors in an Industry's Competitive Structure**

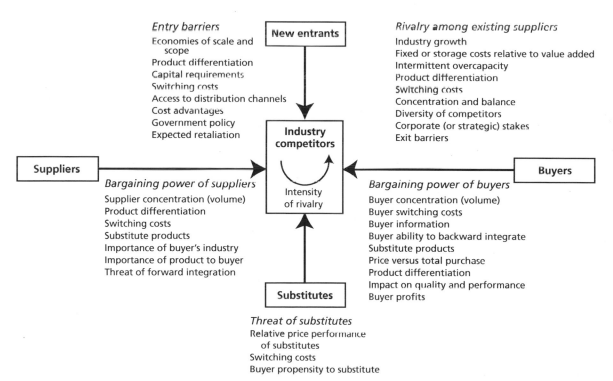

SOURCE: Adapted with permission from Porter, 1983, p. 2.
RAND MG473-3.1

overview of the industry will narrow down the relevant issues that should be pursued with a more detailed analysis. For example, if the broad industry overview reveals an industry with significant entry barriers, then further efforts may focus on identifying the types and sources of the barriers. The investigation may reveal that barriers to entry are due to significant economies of scale from batch production processes, which in turn may indicate that a buyer can negotiate discounts for larger purchases.

**Entry Barriers**

Entry barriers are factors that limit the ability of suppliers to enter the industry. An industry that has few or minor barriers to entry has more actual or potential competition. An industry can be competitive because there are several (or many) suppliers providing a homogeneous good or service. Alternatively, there may be only a few suppliers but extensive potential competition from the threat of additional suppliers entering the industry. Market research should address whether conditions exist that restrict the entry of suppliers into the industry and so limit competition. A limited number of (actual or potential) suppliers can lead to higher prices, create a relationship between the quantity of a product purchased and the price (i.e., buyers who need or who can afford to purchase larger quantities may be eligible for per-unit price reductions), limit product availability (i.e., supply) through limited production capacity, and lock buyers into certain suppliers and products. Table 3.1 lists key issues that market research personnel should look out for when analyzing barriers to entry for an industry. We discuss key issues relating to entry barriers below and how they affect competition and sourcing.

*Economies of scale and scope* are the decreases in the supplier's unit costs that occur when greater quantities are produced.[3] A related factor, economies of scope, measures synergies in production costs of two separate products. Economies of scope exist if the supplier's incremental costs of producing the second product (in conjunction with the first product) are lower than the stand-alone costs of producing only the second product. The lower production costs due to economies of scale or scope can give larger incumbent suppliers a significant cost advantage, thereby limiting the ability of new entrants to compete effectively and subsequently increasing prices and reducing supply. Economies of scale may also indicate the presence of price-volume discounts available to buyers because higher quantities purchased (and hence produced) result in lower average costs per unit.

*Product differentiation* measures customer loyalty generated from actual or perceived differences in characteristics of the good or service. These differences may arise from actual product differences (e.g., specifications, capabilities, or quality), first-mover advantage,[4] effective advertising, brand identity, or attractive customer service. Buyer loyalty generated by product differentiation limits entry because buyers may be less willing (or may be perceived to be less willing) to consider suppliers who are new to the industry. If the actual differences in the

---

[3]  A *minimum efficient scale* limits entry by requiring certain production levels.

[4]  *First-mover advantage* refers to the benefits of being the first producer/seller of a technology (or process) and can comprise cost reductions due to experience or intangible benefits (e.g., reputation as an industry leader).

good or service are important to the buyer's end product, then the buyer may be locked in to a specific supplier. It is important that market research identify potential lock-in (before source selection) because it can affect current and future sourcing opportunities.

*Capital requirements* are resource investments necessary to enter a market that, if substantial, may restrict new entry. These requirements may include physical entry requirements such as tooling or plant facilities or nonproduction expenses on advertising to establish brand identity. Similar to economies of scale, capital requirements can benefit incumbent suppliers and thereby reduce the number of actual and potential suppliers. These requirements also create a relationship between costs and production volume because many of these costs are invariant to production volume and so increasing production levels reduces average cost per unit.

*Switching costs* are tangible and intangible elements that prevent the buyer from choosing to purchase a different good or service or choosing a different supplier. These costs bind the buyer to a particular supplier or product. Key issues include compatibility costs with respect to product redesign, the cost of ancillary products, training employees, the time and effort needed for the buyer to "qualify" the new supplier, and the psychological costs of severing a close supplier relationship. Such costs increase the total cost of the new supplier's product and thereby restrict the willingness and/or ability of buyers to switch to new suppliers. If buyers are locked in (or otherwise committed) to the same suppliers because of substantial switching costs, the industry is less attractive to new suppliers. Switching costs and a limited number of suppliers can affect prices and availability. It is important that switching costs are identified as early as possible because they affect current and future sourcing opportunities.

*Access to distribution channels* measures the ability of a supplier to secure distribution for a product. Difficulties in securing distribution channels reduce the probability that the supplier will enter the industry by imposing substantial costs to new entrants. In turn, this can affect the price, availability, and delivery.

*Cost advantages* are factors (other than economies of scale and scope) that favorably influence costs for certain suppliers. These factors may be related to inputs used in production, labor, proprietary information, or other cost-related factors such as government subsidies. Cost advantages favoring the incumbent suppliers limit the ability of new entrants to compete effectively on price and hence limit entry and, potentially, supply. Cost advantages may also lead to differential pricing across suppliers.

*Government policy* can take the form of explicit limitations and regulation (e.g., licensing or taxes) or implicit restrictions (e.g., environmental standards or limits regarding pollution). These barriers can limit entry if they impose limits on the number of producers or levels of production or if they substantially increase the costs of production. Buyers may be affected through higher prices, limited supply, or limited choice of suppliers.

*Expected retaliation* consists of actions taken by incumbent suppliers to deter new entry or to drive new entrants out of the market. These actions are undertaken by incumbent suppliers to increase or maintain market share (or profits). Antitrust legislation limits some retaliatory behavior (e.g., predatory pricing and collusion), but commitment to an industry or slow growth in an industry incentivizes incumbents to retaliate as they seek to protect their position in the industry. Successful retaliation can limit entry, thereby affecting supply and prices.

**Table 3.1**
**Entry Barriers**

| Factors | Key Issues | Examples | Market Research Data Sources |
|---|---|---|---|
| Economies of scale and scope | Decreases in costs associated with production volume | Change in average or unit cost associated with number of items produced (e.g., cost per unit produced) Minimum efficient scale | Industry reports Trade journals Annual reports |
| | Cost synergies in production of two products | Incremental production costs below stand-alone production costs Intangible know-how in production synergies Brand identity Shared resources | |
| Capital requirements | Large fixed or sunk costs | Facility costs (e.g., plants) Tooling and equipment costs Costs of specific assets (e.g., nonsalable[a]) Research and development costs Advertising expenditures | Industry reports Trade journals Annual reports |
| Switching costs | Product differences | Quality differences Specification differences Capability differences | Industry reports Supplier Web sites and catalogs Trade journals |
| | Lock-in (of costs) | Ancillary costs (e.g., equipment, tooling, and modifications) Product redesign | |
| | Transition costs | Transaction costs Shopping costs (e.g., search costs) Negotiation costs | |
| | Intangible costs | Learning costs (e.g., training) Qualification costs (e.g., certification) Psychological costs of severing a relationship | |
| Access to distribution channels | Access to retail and wholesale distribution networks | Proprietary relationships with key distributors | Industry reports Trade journals Supplier Web sites |
| | Transportation | Access to transportation systems | |
| Cost advantages | Advantages with respect to labor | Learning and/or experience curve Technical expertise | Industry reports Supplier Web sites and annual reports Trade journals Government reports |
| | Advantages with respect to inputs | Favorable access to inputs or factors of production Production of inputs | |
| | Proprietary information | Proprietary technology Patents on tooling and products | |
| | Other cost advantages | Favorable location Government subsidies | |
| Government policy | Regulations | Product standards (e.g., health and safety) Process standards (e.g., environmental pollution) | Government publications Industry reports Trade journals |
| | Restrictions | Licensing Limits on access (e.g., raw materials) Patents (e.g., products, tooling, and patents terms) | |
| | Financial policies | Subsidies/taxes | |

**Table 3.1—Continued**

| Factors | Key Issues | Examples | Market Research Data Sources |
|---------|-----------|----------|------------------------------|
| Expected retaliation | Industry commitment | Asset specificity (e.g., nonsalable assets[a]) Industry growth (e.g., static industry size) Resources (e.g., excess capacity and financial) | Industry reports Trade journals Legal cases |
|  | Anticompetitive behavior | Response to entry (e.g., price cuts) |  |

SOURCE: Adapted from Porter, 1980.

[a] These assets are very specific to a particular production process and so are very difficult to sell for much value; assets that can be used by different industries are easier to sell off and so have lower lock-in.

## The Threat of Substitutes

Substitutes are defined in terms of function. The existence of an alternative product providing suitable functionality can serve as an important deterrent to uncompetitive outcomes (e.g., higher prices or limited supply). A good example is metal containers. Metal containers may be the preferred packaging used by the buyers. However, if the price of metal containers increases substantially, buyers may consider alternative container types. Potential substitutes include glass or plastic containers. Defining the market simply as metal containers neglects the significant competitive pressures from feasible substitutes. The threat of substitutes indicates the extent to which substitute products may affect the market for a particular product. The availability of feasible substitutes can reduce prices for metal containers, improve product quality, and reduce buyer lock-in. But there are limitations. To the extent that glass containers are more expensive to package and ship, small increases in the price of metal containers will not induce substitution. It is the relative performance of the products in key performance areas that determines the feasibility of switching. The following key issues determine the credibility of the threat of substitutes (see also Table 3.2).

*Relative price performance of substitutes* measures how well the substitute performs the desired function given its cost. For example, glass containers may be less expensive in price than metal containers but require more packaging to ensure delivery and may be more costly to ship. These performance and cost factors determine the attractiveness of a substitute product and its ability to affect competition and, therefore, prices, quality, delivery, and other key performance indicators.

*Switching costs* measure the cost to the buyer of changing to a new supplier or product. Costs may be tangible, such as those involved in replacing ancillary components, or intangible (e.g., experience with a product). High switching costs limit the attractiveness of substitutes and their ability to enhance competition because the high switching costs increase the probability that a buyer will stay committed to an existing supplier. Market research should identify potential for lock-in because this affects current and future sourcing opportunities.

**Table 3.2**
**Threat of Substitutes**

| Factors | Key Issues | Examples | Market Research Data Sources |
|---|---|---|---|
| Relative price performance of substitutes | Performance of substitutes relative to cost | Relative prices of substitutes<br>Relative costs of substitutes<br>Relative functional performance (e.g., quality and capabilities) | Industry reports<br>Trade journals<br>Supplier Web sites |
| Switching costs | Monetary costs associated with switching | New tooling<br>Tooling modifications<br>Production changes<br>Product redesign | Trade journals<br>Industry reports<br>Supplier Web sites |
| | Nonmonetary costs associated with switching | Learning (e.g., training)<br>Transition time | |
| Buyer propensity to substitute | Willingness or barriers to switching | Brand identity<br>Customer loyalty (e.g., satisfaction) | Industry reports<br>Trade journals |

SOURCE: Adapted from Porter, 1980.

*Buyer propensity to substitute* measures the willingness of the buyer to turn to a substitute. Intangibles such as brand identity and customer loyalty may reduce the propensity to substitute.

## The Bargaining Power of Suppliers

Supplier bargaining power measures the ability of the supplier to influence prices (or other characteristics) of the market. Supplier power is the inverse of buyer power and consequently many of the factors described here will appear in the "Bargaining Power of Buyers" subsection later in this chapter. Supplier power may allow suppliers to affect prices, create buyer lock-in, and increase demand for their product. Key issues associated with supplier bargaining power are described below and listed in Table 3.3.

**Table 3.3**
**Bargaining Power of Suppliers**

| Factors | Key Issues | Examples | Market Research Data Sources |
|---|---|---|---|
| Supplier concentration (volume) | Industry structure | Size of suppliers (relative to buyer) | Industry report<br>Supplier Web sites<br>Annual reports |
| | Industry concentration | Number of suppliers<br>Distribution of capacity and production<br>Fringe vs. leaders<br>Herfindahl Index[a] | |
| | Industry stability | New entry<br>Recent exits<br>Mergers | |

**Table 3.3—Continued**

| Factors | Key Issues | Examples | Market Research Data Sources |
|---|---|---|---|
| Product differentiation | Proprietary design | Engineering designs<br>Patents on product<br>Patents on tooling/technology | Supplier Web sites (and catalogs)<br>Industry reports<br>Trade journals |
| | Product differences | Quality differences<br>Specification differences<br>Capability differences | |
| | Brand identity and customer loyalty | Market leaders vs. generics<br>Advertising expenditures<br>First-mover advantage | |
| | Customer service | Post-sales service<br>Technical assistance | |
| Switching costs | Product differences | Quality differences<br>Specification differences<br>Capability differences | Industry reports<br>Supplier Web sites and catalogs<br>Trade journals |
| | Lock-in (costs) | Ancillary costs (e.g., equipment, tooling, and modifications)<br>Product redesign | |
| | Transition costs | Transaction costs<br>Shopping costs (e.g., search costs)<br>Negotiation costs | |
| | Intangible costs | Learning costs (e.g., training)<br>Qualification costs (e.g., certification)<br>Psychological costs of severing relationship | |
| Substitute products | Availability of substitutes | Price trade-off<br>Cost trade-off<br>Reliability/quality trade-off | Industry reports<br>Trade journals<br>Competitors |
| Importance of buyer's industry | Value of buyer industry | Percentage of supplier or industry sales<br>Percentage of supplier or industry revenue | Industry reports<br>Annual reports |
| Importance of product to buyer | Buyer end-product quality dependent on input | Specifications (e.g., unique capabilities or technical precision)<br>Quality (e.g., durability)<br>Job stop effect (e.g., oil mining equipment) | Industry reports (from the buyer's industry)<br>Internal personnel |
| Threat of forward integration | Supplier ability (to make/in-source buyer end product) | Technical capabilities<br>Technological similarities<br>Production or process similarities<br>Access to inputs<br>Excess production capacity | Annual reports<br>Industry reports |

SOURCE: Adapted from Porter, 1980.

[a] The Herfindahl Index is a measure of industry concentration among suppliers that is calculated as the sum of squared production shares.

*Supplier concentration (volume)* measures the relative size of suppliers to buyers. This depends, in part, on the number of suppliers in an industry. In isolation, a higher concentration of volume among a few suppliers may indicate that one or more suppliers are able to influence prices, availability, or other terms. But relative size also matters. Large suppliers who sell to smaller buyers have more bargaining power than smaller suppliers (holding buyer size constant) and more bargaining power than suppliers selling to larger buyers. The relative size of suppliers is critical because, if the buyer's purchase represents a minimal purchase, suppliers have little incentive to accommodate the buyer's terms on price or other key performance characteristics. New entry or the threat of new entry will affect this factor.

*Product differentiation* limits the ability of buyers to switch suppliers because the suppliers' products are not perfect substitutes. Competition is enhanced by product homogeneity but reduced by product differentiation (i.e., heterogeneity). Product differentiation is integral to creating buyer lock-in and may take the form of brand identity or differences in customer service, specifications, capabilities, or quality.

*Switching costs* for the buyer increase supplier power through buyer lock-in, while switching costs for the supplier increase buyer leverage. Switching costs can include ancillary products necessary to utilize the new product, training for employees, redesign to the buyer's end product, or psychological costs of severing a close supplier relationship. These costs limit the willingness of the buyer to change suppliers, thereby affecting supply and pricing.

*Substitute products* can limit supplier leverage because these substitutes offer the buyer viable alternative inputs to the supplier's product. In effect, substitutes increase the number of suppliers and supply. A supplier whose product does not have a viable substitute has relatively more power over buyers to influence the terms of a purchase.

*Importance of buyer's industry* limits the extent to which suppliers can leverage their bargaining power. If suppliers rely heavily on the buyer's industry for most of their sales and/or revenue, then they must take into consideration the long-term financial health of the buyers during the procurement process. The buyer's financial health may be dependent not only on the price, but also on quality and other terms of the purchase.

*Importance of product to buyer* creates supplier power. If the supplier's product is integral to the production of the buyer's end product (or integral to its pricing, quality, etc.), there is buyer dependence on the supplier. This creates opportunities for the supplier to influence the terms of the purchase.

*Threat of forward integration* by the supplier indicates that the supplier has the ability (e.g., capacity and capability) to produce the buyer's end product. This ability creates supplier power because the supplier can become another end user and thereby generate demand (and hence price increases) for his own (input) product. He can also compete with the buyer in the market for the end product.

## Rivalry Among Existing Suppliers

Rivalry among suppliers measures the intensity of competition. Determinants of rivalry speak to the extent to which suppliers must compete with each other for the same customers, thereby affecting prices, availability of supply, quality, and other terms. The key issues associated with rivalry are described below and listed in Table 3.4.

*Industry growth* measures the increase in demand (sometimes measured as production volume or sales) over time. Industry growth eases rivalry because all suppliers can, in principle,

**Table 3.4**
**Market Rivalry**

| Factors | Key Issues | Examples | Market Research Data Sources |
|---|---|---|---|
| Industry growth | Supplier growth due to market growth or market share | Change in market size (demand)<br>Change in capacity and usage<br>Change in distribution of supplier shares (e.g., Herfindahl Index[a]) | Annual reports<br>Industry reports<br>Trade journals |
| Fixed or storage costs vs. value added (e.g., low margins) | Fixed costs relative to value added<br>Storage costs relative to value added | Fixed costs to value added ratio<br>Storage costs to value added ratio | Industry reports<br>Annual reports |
| Intermittent overcapacity | Excess capacity and demand variability | Demand vs. production capacity<br>Periodic or recent layoffs<br>Periodic or recent plant closings<br>Nature of production augmentation (e.g., scale of new plants)<br>New plant openings<br>New entry<br>New supplier technology<br>Declining industry (e.g., negative growth)<br>Demand forecasts<br>Buyer technology, processes, or products<br>Shortages (e.g., backorders or fill rates)<br>Extra shifts or temporary labor<br>Layoffs | Newspapers<br>Annual reports<br>Industry reports<br>Trade journals |
| Product differentiation | Proprietary design | Engineering designs<br>Patents on product<br>Patents on tooling or technology | Supplier Web sites (and catalogs)<br>Industry reports<br>Trade journals |
| | Product differences | Quality differences<br>Specification differences<br>Capability differences | |
| | Brand identity and customer loyalty | Market leaders vs. generics<br>Advertising expenditures<br>First-mover advantage | |
| | Customer service | Post-sales service<br>Technical assistance | |
| Switching costs | Product differences | Quality differences<br>Specification differences<br>Capability differences | Industry reports<br>Supplier Web sites and catalogs<br>Trade journals |
| | Lock-in (of costs) | Ancillary costs (e.g., equipment, tooling, or modifications)<br>Product redesign | |
| | Transition costs | Transaction costs<br>Shopping costs (e.g., search costs)<br>Negotiation costs | |
| | Intangible costs | Learning costs (e.g., training)<br>Qualification costs (e.g., certification)<br>Psychological costs of severing relationship | |
| Concentration and balance | Distribution of supplier influence within an industry | Distribution of production<br>Herfindahl Index[a]<br>Number and size of leading suppliers | Industry reports<br>Supplier Web sites<br>Annual reports |

**Table 3.4—Continued**

| Factors | Key Issues | Examples | Market Research Data Sources |
|---------|-----------|----------|------------------------------|
| Diversity of competitors | Differences and similarities in corporate strategy of individual suppliers | Supplier key market segments (e.g., low-cost, high-quality, geographic, and niche markets) | Annual reports<br>Supplier Web sites<br>Industry reports |
| Corporate (or strategic) stakes | Importance of industry to supplier | Share of volume purchased by industry<br>Corporate strategy<br>Effect on overall profitability<br>Effect on other segments | Annual reports<br>Supplier Web sites<br>Industry reports |
| Exit barriers | Economic and strategic | Asset specificity (e.g., nonsalable assets[b])<br>Liquidation value<br>Cost of modifications (for other use)<br>Labor agreements<br>Resettlement costs<br>Spare parts availability<br>Economies of scope (e.g., production synergies across products)<br>Brand identity<br>Access to financial markets<br>Shared facilities | Industry reports<br>Trade journals<br>Government reports |
| | Government/regulatory | Government restrictions to exit | |
| | Emotional | Attachment to an industry<br>Loyalty to employees<br>Career concerns (e.g., stigma) | |

SOURCE: Adapted from Porter, 1980.

[a] The Herfindahl Index is a measure of industry concentration among suppliers that is calculated as the sum of squared production shares.

[b] These assets are very specific to a particular production process and so are very difficult to sell for much value; assets that can be used by different industries are easier to sell off and so have lower lock-in.

increase sales and revenue (and, potentially, profits) without having to capture a competitor's market share. In turn, growth eases competition for buyers on prices and other purchase terms.

*Fixed or storage costs relative to value added* measure the margins associated with production. Specifically, this measure identifies the value added by the supplier to the product relative to the costs associated with production and storage. Low margins can increase rivalry as suppliers increase production or lower prices in order to ensure sales.

*Intermittent overcapacity* is common in industries in which capacity or production is added in large segments (e.g., new plants or batch production) or in which demand is cyclical. Intermittent overcapacity increases rivalry among suppliers seeking to utilize capacity by attracting and retaining buyers. This rivalry can yield better sourcing terms for the buyer because the supplier may be willing to negotiate to ensure demand.

*Product differentiation* indicates that suppliers' products are heterogeneous rather than homogeneous. Homogeneity intensifies competition on price because there is little difference in products to induce customer loyalty. Heterogeneity can reduce competition for buyers by segmenting buyers based on product characteristics (e.g., quality or specifications). Actual or perceived product differences can affect price and sourcing efforts by creating lock-in.

*Switching costs* measure the costs incurred by buyers to switch suppliers. These can include the cost of ancillary products, training costs, and product redesign. Significant switching costs limit rivalry because small price differences are not sufficient to induce buyers to switch suppliers. Switching costs can lock the buyer into a specific product or supplier thereby limiting sourcing options.

*Concentration and balance* influence rivalry among suppliers. A greater number of suppliers or greater equality among suppliers as measured by production volume or other measures of influence enhances competition for buyers and can improve buyer terms (e.g., reduced prices).

*Diversity of competitors* affects rivalry because diverse competitors will not be following the same strategy. An industry with two suppliers following divergent competitive strategies will have less intense rivalry than an industry in which both suppliers pursue the same strategy. For example, if two suppliers compete for the same customers by both pursuing a low-price strategy, rivalry is more intense than if each supplier pursued different market segments or niches (e.g., low price versus high quality).

*Corporate (or strategic) stakes* increase rivalry. If suppliers feel that a market segment is a key element of their corporate strategy, then rivalry for that segment (i.e., those buyers) will be intense, with suppliers offering favorable terms to contested buyers.

*Exit barriers* are economic, strategic, emotional, and government factors that limit the ability of the supplier to exit the industry. In some cases, these factors create costs to exit that exceed the losses incurred by remaining in the industry. With limited options for exit, suppliers are more bound to success within the market and hence will compete more intensely. Exit barriers can reduce prices, affect output levels, and influence other terms.

## Bargaining Power of Buyers

Thus far, the focus has been on the supply side. But buyer power is also important. To the extent that buyers have more leverage than suppliers, they are able to negotiate lower prices or other concessions. A buyer whose purchases constitute a significant portion of the industry's production capacity (or sales) or of a particular supplier's capacity (or sales) can leverage this fact in the negotiation process.[5] The factors described below and in Table 3.5 determine whether buyers are able to influence the terms of procurement, including prices, delivery, quality, warranty, and other terms of the purchase.

*Buyer concentration (volume)* reflects the size of the buyer's purchase relative to supplier sales. The larger the buyer, the more important its business to the supplier and the greater its ability to influence contract terms (e.g., prices).

---

[5] However, the buyer should never be too large a share of a supplier's production (or sales), to avoid dependence.

**Table 3.5**
**Bargaining Power of Buyers**

| Factors | Key Issues | Examples | Market Research Data Sources |
|---|---|---|---|
| Buyer concentration (volume) | Industry structure | Size of buyers (relative to suppliers) | Industry report Supplier Web sites Annual reports |
| | Industry concentration | Number of buyers Distribution of capacity and production Fringe vs. leaders Herfindahl Index[a] | |
| | Industry stability | New entry Recent exits Mergers | |
| Switching costs | Product differences | Quality differences Specification differences Capability differences | Industry reports Supplier Web sites and catalogs Trade journals |
| | Lock-in (costs) | Ancillary costs (e.g., equipment, tooling, and modifications) Product redesign | |
| | Transition costs | Transaction costs Shopping costs (e.g., search costs) Negotiation costs | |
| | Intangible costs | Learning costs (e.g., training) Qualification costs (e.g., certification) Psychological costs of severing relationship | |
| Buyer information | Information on the supplier's business | Demand for product Actual prices (e.g., for other buyers) Supplier costs (e.g., inputs, labor, and advertising) | Industry reports Supplier Web sites Competitors Colleagues |
| Buyer ability to backward integrate | Buyer capability (to make/in-source) Buyer capacity (to make/in-source) | Technical capabilities Technological similarities Production similarities Access to inputs Excess production capacity | Annual reports Industry reports Supplier Web sites |
| Substitute products | Availability of substitutes | Price trade-off Reliability/quality trade-off | Industry reports Trade journals Competitors |
| Price vs. total purchase | Cost importance of input | Input price relative to total cost of end product | Industry reports Trade journals Spend analyses |
| Product differentiation | Proprietary design | Engineering designs Patents on products Patents on tooling or technology | Supplier Web sites (and catalogs) Industry reports Trade journals |
| | Product differences | Quality differences Specification differences Capability differences | |
| | Brand identity and customer loyalty | Market leaders vs. generics Advertising expenditures First-mover advantage | |
| | Customer service | Post-sales service Technical assistance | |

**Table 3.5—Continued**

| Factors | Key Issues | Examples | Market Research Data Sources |
|---|---|---|---|
| Effect on quality and performance | Buyer end-product quality dependent on input | Specifications (e.g., unique capabilities or technical precision)<br>Quality (e.g., durability)<br>Job stop effect (e.g., for oil mining equipment) | Industry reports<br>Trade journals<br>Internal analyses and personnel |
| Buyer profits | Buyer financial performance | Profit margins<br>Industry profits | Annual reports<br>Industry reports<br>Internal analyses |

SOURCE: Adapted from Porter, 1980.

[a] The Herfindahl Index is a measure of industry concentration among suppliers that is calculated as the sum of squared production shares.

*Buyer switching costs* are tangible and intangible costs associated with switching to a new supplier. Few or minimal switching costs increase buyer bargaining power, while substantial costs that bind the buyer to an existing supplier limit buyer power. Lock-in resulting from switching costs can affect current and future sourcing options.

*Buyer information* concerning demand, actual market prices, supplier costs, and contacts with other buyers provides the buyer with the ability to negotiate more-favorable terms. In essence, market research may allow the buyer to influence prices and other contract terms.

*Buyer ability to backward integrate* indicates that buyers have the ability to produce their own inputs as an alternative to purchasing from suppliers, thereby increasing their bargaining position relative to suppliers.[6] By producing the input, the buyer can increase availability and influence prices.

*Substitute products* are products that provide a functional alternative to the original product. The existence of suitable substitutes is akin to increasing the number of suppliers. As a result, substitutes may reduce prices. However, the effect of substitutes can be limited by differences in functionality, higher prices, and ancillary costs (e.g., shipping).

*Price versus total purchase* determines the buyer's price sensitivity. If the price of an input product represents a minor element in the buyer's total costs of purchased materials, the buyer is likely to be less sensitive to the cost.

*Product differentiation* indicates that the product is heterogeneous, while a lack of product differentiation indicates a homogenous product. Homogeneity increases the ability of the buyer to turn to and/or leverage alternative suppliers during negotiations, thereby increasing buyer bargaining power. Brand identity, perceived and actual product differences (e.g., specifications and capabilities), and differences in aftermarket support (e.g., customer service) are indicators of product differentiation that limit buyer power through lock-in.

---

[6]  Appendix B details the make-versus-buy decision.

*Effect on quality and performance* of the input on the buyer's end product may limit price sensitivity and bargaining power. Buyers are frequently tied to an input that plays a vital role in the quality or performance of the buyer's end product. This reliance tends to limit their bargaining ability.

*Buyer profits* are related to price sensitivity. Buyers with strong profits tend to be less price-sensitive and are less prone to cost-cutting measures.

## Benchmark the Industry Standards and Norms

The next step is to benchmark the industry standards and norms. Industry standards relate to product standards and supplier performance. Product standards can be used to evaluate the potential for standardization to increase the pool of potential suppliers. Benchmarking of key performance indicators, such as typical defect rates, provides necessary background information for assessing the performance of individual suppliers. Research on industry norms can inform such purchasing practices as contract lengths and price-volume discounts, issues with respect to industry financial performance, and the relevance of the macroeconomic environment to the industry.

### Industry Standards

Industry standards are important for understanding what to expect from the industry. They include product specifications, production processes, quality, and technology. These benchmarks are useful for understanding the industry and later for evaluating individual suppliers (see Chapter Five). Specific issues of interest related to these standards are listed in Table 3.6.

**Table 3.6**
**Industry Standards**

| Factors | Key Issues | Examples | Market Research Data Sources |
|---------|-----------|----------|------------------------------|
| Specifications and standardization | Compatibility and specifications | Availability of standardized products<br>Cost of modifications<br>Lock-in | Internal sources (e.g., engineering)<br>Competitors<br>Industry reports |
| Quality | Reliability | Defect rate<br>Mean time between failures<br>Quality controls (e.g., inspections)<br>Certification<br>Customer satisfaction | Internal sources (e.g., supplier database)<br>Supplier Web sites<br>References<br>Industry reports<br>Trade journals |
| Production | Production process | Batch<br>Continuous<br>Periodic | Industry reports |
| Technology | Maturity and adoption | Obsolescence<br>Compatibility<br>Rate of adoption<br>Rate of innovation<br>Years since adoption | Industry reports<br>Trade journals<br>Supplier Web sites |

*Specifications and standardization* are necessary in order to understand how the purchase requirements fit into the industry standards. The buyer's purchase requirements and specifications should be reviewed to determine whether they comply with industry standards for that product. If not, commodity teams must determine whether the modifications to the product are necessary. If not, then staff must consider whether the modifications can be reduced or eliminated to ensure that the purchase can be competitively sourced. Product standardization is a common and effective mechanism for reducing costs. Proliferation of part numbers is a recognized cost driver that should be minimized (especially, in the design stage). Standardization not only reduces the costs to the current supplier, but also opens the sourcing process to a larger number of potential suppliers. Standardization is key to reducing costs, avoiding lock-in, ensuring availability, and enhancing competition. If a standard product can be used effectively in place of a customized product, the cost savings can be substantial. The analysis of requirements and specifications is common among commercial enterprises, but is also required by recent Department of Defense regulations, which require the use of nondevelopment and commercial items whenever possible. The following questions are relevant to this analysis:[7]

- Do the product requirements, specifications, and capabilities conform to industry standards?
- Are there standard products (or substitutes) in inventory or available in the market that provide the same functionality?
- Are all the requirements, specifications, and capabilities *necessary* to the product's function? Which (if any) requirements, specifications, or capabilities can be eliminated or modified to adhere to industry standards (without sacrificing the necessary functionality)?
- How have the specifications and functions changed over time? How are they expected to change?

*Quality* is a related issue. What degree of performance on quality should the buyer expect from the industry? Information on quality metrics, such as mean times between failures and defect rates, will help the buyer understand the quality of its own end product and what, if any, redesigns should be undertaken. The investigation will also determine whether third-party quality certifications (e.g., ISO-9000) are common.

*Production* information is useful in understanding pricing and availability. For example, batch production processes may mean that smaller orders are more costly or that the industry may be less responsive to unexpected changes in demand.

*Technology* may be a critical factor for some industries in understanding the market and how it may change in the future. For example, a high rate of technological change can indicate that the price of a product is trending downward so that indexing the price paid is more appropriate than locking in to a fixed price for an extended period. This was the case with computer

---

[7] This list assumes that initial questions with respect to the development of the sourcing strategy—such as the make-or-buy decision—have already been addressed. Additional detail can be found in Appendix B.

memory in the 1990s. Alternatively, a high rate of technological change among emerging suppliers will help determine whether the current top suppliers are innovating quickly enough to maintain their current position

### Industry Norms

Industry norms are common practices or characteristics of the industry (see Table 3.7). We focus on purchasing practices, financial performance, and the effects of the macroeconomic environment, but other areas may also apply. The industry overview should reveal the broad characteristics of interest.

*Purchasing practices* are industry norms relating to the procurement process. These can include norms for contract terms and pricing practices. Contract terms include the use of particular contract types (e.g., fixed price versus cost plus), the average length of the contract, and other terms, including options years and warranties. Pricing practices include price-volume discounts that may be common in the industry and pricing for production versus aftermarket or support parts.

**Table 3.7**
**Industry Norms**

| Factors | Key Issues | Examples | Market Research Data Sources |
|---|---|---|---|
| Purchasing practices | Contract terms | Type of contract (e.g., fixed price or cost plus) Average length and terms | Internal sources Industry reports |
| | Pricing practices | Volume discounts | |
| | Customer support | Parts availability Technical assistance Warranty terms | |
| Financial performance | Profitability | Profit margins (e.g., supplier and industry) Revenue and expenses | Industry reports Annual reports Third-party observers (e.g., D&B) |
| | Financial stability | Historical profits, revenues, and expenses Financial indicators[a] | |
| | Risks | Bankruptcy Failure to deliver Layoffs and plant closings Inability to purchase inputs (e.g., credit issues) | |
| Macroeconomic environment | Cyclicality and performance under particular economic conditions | Seasonal and holiday variation Economic cycle (e.g., procyclical vs. countercyclical)[b] | Government Web sites Industry reports |

[a] See Appendix D for specific financial indicators, resources for data, and interpretation of indicators.

[b] Procyclical industries experience greater demand during general economic expansions, while countercyclical industries experience greater demand during general economic recessions.

*Financial performance* is important in that it indicates the state of the industry. Is the industry financially sound? How variable is financial performance? Does financial instability or variability indicate potential risks for the buyer? The financial performance of an industry is of interest in its own right. However, such information will also be useful in assessing the relative performance of individual suppliers (see more about evaluating a supplier's financial strength in Chapter Five).

*Macroeconomic environment* can affect both industry and supplier performance. It is important to understand how general macroeconomic conditions affect the industry. Are industry sales and profits procyclical in that they increase during general expansions and decline during recessions? Or are they countercyclical? How do general macroeconomic conditions affect other measures of industry performance? Do industry costs increase as a result of labor cost increases during expansions? Are there any other cycles—such as seasons or holidays—that affect the industry? Such analyses can explain changes in industry performance and highlight how changing economic conditions will affect future performance.

## Analyze Price and Cost

The price and TCO of goods and services is fundamental to purchasing decisions and to market research. But what is the difference between price and TCO? The purchase (or selling) price is what the supplier charges a buyer for a good or service. For some goods and services, the price is equivalent to TCO. For others, price is not even the most critical component of TCO. TCO encompasses all costs incurred by the buyer before, during, and after the transaction. This information is critical to selecting the appropriate product and supplier and can also be useful in the negotiation process.[8]

### Conducting a Should-Cost Analysis

The first step to developing an understanding of the elements of supplier costs is to understand what a product should cost and build an estimate of what the selling price should be. A should-cost analysis is an analysis of the selling price based on the necessary inputs to production, the price of inputs, overhead costs, and the industry norms on profitability. Market research on the industry should identify key cost drivers for an industry and highlight issues associated with supplier costs. Table 3.8 provides a list of key issues and sample cost drivers. Information on the key cost drivers may be found in industry reports, government data, trade journals, supplier data, and supplier annual reports.

---

[8]  Software packages are available to assist in calculating these analyses.

There are a number of specific techniques, including bottom-up analysis, cost-estimating relationships, and reasoning by analogy (Younossi et al., 2003). Bottom-up analysis is a detailed and intensive pricing of individual components similar to a "should-cost" analysis. The cost-estimating-relationship and reasoning-by-analogy techniques rely on previous experience with purchasing similar types of goods and services. However, these two techniques are most useful when the previous purchases used to evaluate costs were themselves rigorously analyzed.

**Table 3.8**
**A Should-Cost Analysis**

| Factor | Key Issues | Examples | Market Research Data Sources |
|--------|-----------|----------|------------------------------|
| Costs | Elements of supplier cost | Wages<br>Inputs prices<br>Capital costs<br>Input supply availability<br>Fringe benefits (e.g., health benefits)<br>Labor issues (e.g., unions, strikes, or collective bargaining agreements)<br>Technological change<br>Transportation (e.g., weight and distance)<br>Packaging and materials<br>Service support<br>Other follow-up costs (e.g., upgrades) | Industry reports<br>Government data (e.g., producer price indexes and employment reports)<br>Trade journals<br>Supplier data<br>Annual reports |
| | Variability in key cost drivers | Price changes and trends<br>Seasonality or cyclicality<br>Changes in expected demand/supply<br>Changes in production processes<br>Technological changes | |

Once the key cost drivers have been identified, it is useful to construct an estimate of what the product should cost. The selling price encompasses three major elements—direct costs, indirect costs, and profit (see Table 3.9 for an example). These elements can be defined as follows (see Leenders et al., 2001):

- **Direct costs** include the costs of inputs in the production process. Inputs include both the materials and labor used to produce the product. Direct costs include only the variable costs—those costs that vary directly with the quantity produced. In essence, it should be possible to attribute these variable costs to a particular production unit.
- **Indirect costs** cannot be allocated to a particular production unit because these costs do not vary directly with each unit. Indirect costs include overhead costs, such as rent, property tax, tooling or machine depreciation, expenses of general supervisors, data processing, and utility costs. There are two main types of indirect costs: semivariable and fixed costs. Semivariable costs vary somewhat with production, but not on an individual unit basis. Other indirect costs are categorized as fixed costs because they do not vary at all with production levels.
- **Profit** is the return to the supplier for his investment in the production process. The industry analysis should provide some support for the rate of profits.

## Conducting a Total-Cost Analysis

It is important to differentiate price from cost. Traditionally, the focus of cost analysis was the calculation of the should-cost or selling price. For homogeneous commodities in a competitive industry, this focus on selling price may still be appropriate. But for many purchases, the TCO to the buyer can be several times the selling price. The selling price is an element of cost, but there are a number of other factors that can drive up the total cost of a purchase. Consequently,

**Table 3.9**
**Example of a Should-Cost Buildup in Manufacturing**

| Factors | Costs | Assumptions |
|---|---|---|
| Direct costs | | |
|    Direct materials | $5,500 | |
|    Direct labor | $2,000 | |
|    Factory overhead (all indirect factory costs, both fixed and variable) | $2,500 | 125 percent of direct labor |
|    Subtotal | $10,000 | |
| Indirect costs | | |
|    General, administrative, and selling costs | $1,500 | 15 percent of manufacturing cost |
|    Subtotal | $11,500 | |
| Profit | $920 | 8 percent of total cost |
| Subtotal | $12,420 | |
| Total: selling price | $12,420 | |

SOURCE: Adapted from Leenders et al., 2001, p. 345. *Purchasing and Supply Management,* 12th ed., © The McGraw-Hill Companies, Inc., 2002. Used by permission.

the product or supplier with the lowest selling price is not necessarily the product with the lowest total cost for the buyer.[9] For example, a critical component of aircraft are engines, for which aftermarket service support may exceed the initial purchase price. In such cases, TCO analysis should be used to assess the total costs of each supplier and product to the enterprise.

By calculating the TCO for each product, the relative costs can be compared. However, the benefits of TCO analyses are not limited to source or product selection. Like cost analysis, TCO can also assist in negotiations with a single supplier and in supplier management. By knowing what a product should cost and knowing its full cost to the enterprise (in isolation and relative to other products), the enterprise is in a more informed bargaining position.

What types of costs might cause total cost to differ substantially from purchase price? TCO includes the life-cycle cost of a good or service, including acquisition, implementation, support, and disposal (Leenders et al., 2001; Burt, Dobler, and Starling, 2003). The most relevant costs in TCO analysis are a function of the industry and the purchase. For example, transportation costs might be critical for fragile or physically heavy purchases. On the other hand, the cost of aftermarket support is key for other products, such as aircraft engines.

This approach divides the costs into three categories based on timing: (1) pre-transaction components, (2) transaction components, and (3) post-transaction components. Figure 3.2 lists key elements of each of these three categories. The pre-transaction costs include the investment—both monetary and nonmonetary—involved in sourcing, such as identifying a need, conducting market research, selecting a supplier, and learning to do business with a sup-

---

[9] The TCO analyses can also be calculated for individual suppliers to compare the relative cost to the buyer across suppliers. This is discussed further in Chapter Five.

**Figure 3.2**
**A TCO Analysis**

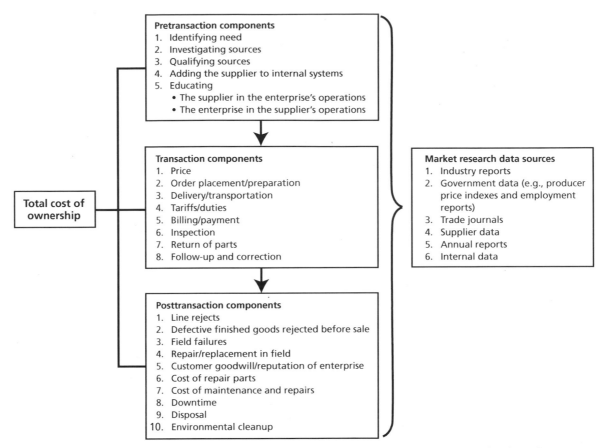

SOURCE: Adapted from Leenders et al., 2001, p. 377 (*Purchasing and Supply Management*, 12th ed., © The McGraw-Hill Companies, Inc., 2002) and Burt, Dobler, and Starling, 2003 (*World Class Supply Management: The Key to Supply Chain Management*, 7th ed., © The McGraw-Hill Companies, Inc., 2003). Both used by permission.
**RAND** *MG473-3.2*

plier. The transaction costs include not only the selling price, but also any other elements that accompany the purchase, such as delivery, government-imposed costs, inspection, and returns. Finally, post-transaction costs include the tangible and intangible burdens that failure on the part of the supplier impose on the enterprise. These costs may affect the enterprise directly through production stoppages and rejections. Or they may affect the enterprise indirectly through decreased customer satisfaction and repairs/returns of the end product. Commercial enterprises estimate the costs of these failures (e.g., defects) to produce an accurate measure of TCO. Based on the TCO analysis, costs may far exceed the "selling price" calculated in the should-cost analysis.

A useful and consistent concept for costs is zero base pricing (ZBP) (Burt, Norquist, and Anklesaria, 1990). Like TCO, ZBP seeks to identify and reduce the enterprise's total costs—which include supplier costs and costs within the enterprise. For the purchase price,

ZBP examines input materials, labor, overhead, general and administrative costs, and profits. Within-enterprise costs examine how the good affects internal costs through transportation, inventory, delivery, and quality factors. In this respect, ZBP is very similar to TCO analysis. ZBP is intended to be a proactive approach that—like the market research outlined in this monograph—examines methods to reduce these costs throughout the sourcing process starting at the design stage. For example, ZBP would examine not only the cost elements, but also look at all issues that may affect costs, such as quality, delivery, inventory, standardization, specifications, and improved information flow (e.g., communication of demand). The process is most effective when there is collaboration between relevant stakeholders at the enterprise and suppliers to identify and reduce costs.

---

**Interview Lessons: Total Cost of Ownership and Consolidation of Contracts**

TCO and ZBP are approaches to assist the enterprise in identifying and controlling all the costs associated with a purchase. The literature emphasizes consolidation of buys across the enterprise and across commodities to maximize leverage, but the enterprises we interviewed sometimes viewed consolidation in even broader terms. The enterprises' spend analyses and market research—including TCO—revealed that aftermarket/support services costs for some products far outweighed the initial purchase price. In response, the enterprises negotiated and signed contracts for aftermarket/support services *at the same time* as the original purchase. This consolidation of purchase and aftermarket/support service agreements was key to avoid being taken advantage of by the supplier. Traditionally, the enterprises had signed purchase agreements and then discussed aftermarket/support service. However, having to negotiate aftermarket/support service after they had already locked in to the product created supplier power and left them at a disadvantage in the negotiations. If the purchase had already taken place, but aftermarket/support service concerns remained, the enterprises found that (in some cases) it was still possible to leverage these legacy items as long as new projects were sourced. These enterprises bundled new contracts with legacy items.

---

The cost analyses outlined here are used not only to calculate costs, but also to control costs and to identify opportunities for cost improvements. When costs increase, the commodity team should consider whether the increases are attributable to changes in key cost drivers and what action can be undertaken to control or reduce costs. To the extent possible, increases in critical and high-value purchases should be examined carefully to determine the extent to which the supplier price and internal cost increases are unavoidable.

For example, a 10 percent increase in the cost for a technology help center may be driven by a surging economy driving up the wages of employees in industries with strong demand. But *how much* of the increased costs are attributable to particular factors? If an analysis of compensation data indicates that wages for computer technicians increased by 5 percent in the previous year, it would explain only half of the 10 percent increase in costs. The remaining 50 percent must be further investigated. Are fringe benefits such as health care costs also increasing? Are other factors such as hardware costs or office rental costs also increasing? In cases for which the costs are justified by increases in supplier costs, the analysis may consider other sourcing issues. What, if any, productivity improvements are possible to offset these increases? Is the decision to source domestically still the appropriate one?

## Investigate the Industry's Past and Anticipate the Future

Analysis of the issues discussed above should not focus solely on a point in time. Trends and projections are equally important in crafting a supply strategy that ensures that the goals of the enterprise are met.

### Looking Back at Trends

Analysis of trends can explain changes in prices, availability, and other key performance metrics. For example, changes in industry structure may explain an upcoming price increase or reductions in availability. Relevant issues include: How has the number of suppliers changed recently because of new entry, exits (e.g., bankruptcies), mergers, and acquisitions? How has total production and capacity changed over time? How has the distribution of capacity changed over time? Do recent exits indicate a shift in supplier power via increased concentration of capacity?

Such questions can be answered only when market research includes a look at trends. Including the past in market research gives the team a broader perspective and highlights any market cycles, such as seasonality, annual events (e.g., year-end clearances), contract renewals, and sensitivity to general economic activity (e.g., recessions). Industry reports are often a useful source for information on trends, especially early in the market research process. However, over time, the enterprise's own market research can help identify the evolution of an industry.

### Projecting the Future

Neither the industry nor the needs of the enterprise are static. For example, the potential for entry or exit in a market and technological innovation among suppliers marks a dynamic process that can affect source selection. Likewise, changes in the enterprise's own production processes may shift its requirements from one product or supplier to another.

Both the current and the projected needs of the enterprise must be compared to the current and projected condition of the market. The typical enterprise considers quality, quantity, delivery, cost, service, and other characteristics in the source selection decision. Each of these characteristics must be evaluated under present and future conditions to ensure that both short-term and long-term considerations are evaluated. Even if the broad characteristics by which the enterprise's requirements and market conditions are evaluated do not change from period to period, market research should examine both the current situation and future scenarios with respect to these characteristics. The analysis of these factors over time can reveal dramatic changes.

The following example highlights the value of this approach (see Leenders and Blenkhorn, 1988). Consider market research and analysis that is conducted for a low-priority item that is currently in abundant supply. Analysis of the current conditions and requirements indicates

**Interview Lessons: Sharing Information with Suppliers**

Projections regarding the enterprise's future needs are useful in carrying out market research. But enterprises also shared information on their current and projected demand with their suppliers. The information was useful in preparing suppliers for increases (or decreases) in demand as well as changes in technology. By sharing the projections with the suppliers, the enterprise allowed suppliers an opportunity to alert the enterprise of any problems in meeting future demand.

that the item under consideration is currently a C item with a reasonable price.[10] The categorization implies that low procurement effort is required. It is a buyer's market when both price and supply are not a concern. However, looking forward reveals that demand within the enterprise is projected to increase markedly, perhaps because the item will be an important input in a new production process. The item will then move from the C to the A category. Both supply and price issues will then become vital. At the same time, this analysis also reveals that the market for this product is changing. What is currently a buyer's market is projected to transform into a seller's market as the new production process increases demand for the item for a number of buyers. In the future, the enterprise will have difficulties securing not only a good price, but also a stable supply of an item that is expected to play a significant role in production.

Although the supply and price concerns are not immediate, they may require that the enterprise begin looking into procurement alternatives immediately. The research and analysis should indicate the time frame for the changing conditions so that the enterprise can make timely changes in its practices. Procurement of the item must change to protect the enterprise. There are several options that should be evaluated. The enterprise may communicate its increased needs (i.e., demand) and enter into a long-term contract with a supplier or increase the number of suppliers for that good or service in its supply base. Another option is "reverse marketing," which is when the enterprise makes an effort to develop a new supplier—perhaps from among existing manufacturers with similar products or processes. Alternatively, the enterprise may consider developing in-house production capabilities to ensure supply. Both reverse marketing and in-house production are much more resource-intensive approaches and so should be restricted to particular situations and after substantial analysis of the costs and benefits.

Procurement analysis comparing only current market conditions and enterprise requirements would not have revealed the upcoming need for change in the procurement process. Of course, it would be difficult to perform such detailed analysis for all items purchased by the enterprise. For items that are currently high value or a potential vulnerability, market research should highlight any future concerns. Also, close contact between the commodity team and other departments within the enterprise can draw attention to particular items of concern.

---

[10] The terminology for Groups A, B, and C are taken from Chapter Two's review of Pareto analysis. Group A items include 10–20 percent of the total products purchased but 70–80 percent of total expenditures. Group B items include 30–50 percent of products purchased but account for only 10–20 percent of expenditures. Group C items include 40–70 percent of products but only 10–20 percent of expenditures. Group A items typically require the most attention, Group B some attention, and Group C the least attention in the market research and sourcing process (subject to an assessment of risk).

For example, the design engineers developing a new production process or new end product should inform the commodity team of any significant upcoming increase in demand. On the procurement side, information about potential interruptions to supply should be passed along to production departments and design teams.

## Summary

### Review: What to Do

This chapter outlined an approach to analyzing the industry with specific focus on how competition affects sourcing, industry standards and norms, and cost analyses. The following summarizes the suggestions and action steps discussed in this chapter.

1. Investigate the competitiveness of the industry with an eye to how competition affects sourcing. The five forces framework (Porter, 1980) identifies key issues for understanding the competitiveness of an industry. The original framework was developed to understand competition, but market research should focus on how competition issues might affect sourcing efforts.
2. Benchmark industry standards and norms.
3. Conduct a cost analysis:
   • Use a should-cost analysis to estimate the selling price of the required good or service.
   • Use a TCO approach to estimate all the costs that the enterprise incurs before, during, and after a purchasing transaction.
4. Identify trends, cycles, and future changes in order to identify and address risks and opportunities.

### Where to Look for Relevant Information

The industry analysis described in this chapter relies on a number of sources including third-party industry observers, periodicals, and suppliers. Most useful sources include the following:

• third-party industry observers
  – government
  – industry
  – academic
  – private sources
  – market intelligence research firms
  – periodicals
  – trade journals (e.g., *Aviation Week*)
  – purchasing journals (e.g., *Purchasing*)
• supplier information
  – annual reports
  – supplier Web sites.

# CHAPTER FOUR

# Identify Potential Suppliers

The next step in the market research process is to identify (or make a list of) potential suppliers.[1] Potential suppliers can include current suppliers, former suppliers, and new suppliers.[2] Current and former suppliers are clear candidates with whom the buyer has previous experience and an understanding of their capabilities and performance. The list should also include new suppliers who have not previously contracted with the enterprise; these suppliers may include new entrants, operate in a different location, or offer functional substitutes.

## Sources of Information

The key to supplier identification is to find and develop good sources of information. Potential sources include the enterprise's own records, suppliers, industry sources, trade organizations, journals, and other resources. In this chapter, we describe potential sources and their strengths and weaknesses. The list of resources in this chapter and their descriptions are adapted from Burt, Dobler, and Starling, 2003; Monczka, Trent, and Handfield, 2001; Raedels, 2000; and Dobler and Burt, 1996. A sample list of specific Internet sources drawn from these and other sources is included in Appendix C.

### Supplier Database[3]

A good place to start is with the current supply base. Enterprises should have compiled information—preferably in an enterprise-wide supplier database—on all suppliers who are currently contracted by the enterprise. This database should be the most accessible source of relevant information for supplier identification. A good supplier database should also contain

---

[1] This process is described for an industry with a number of suppliers, but some industries may have limited competition.

[2] There may also be some cases in which all existing suppliers for a product do not meet the needs of the buyer. In these cases, the enterprise may also consider "nontraditional" suppliers. These suppliers do not yet provide the desired good or service. Rather, they produce goods or services using similar technologies or processes and so may be willing to undertake a new good or service. This process requires supplier development activity and perhaps some investment (e.g., tooling or training)—which can be costly. Clearly, the use of supplier development activities (or reverse marketing) is dependent on the projected costs and benefits. We discuss supplier development activities briefly in Chapter Six.

[3] Supplier databases have replaced traditional supplier information files.

information on former suppliers—those who have been contracted in the past. Potential suppliers in the database include suppliers with whom the enterprise has had previous experience either with the good or service in question or with similar goods and services.

The database may also provide information regarding new suppliers. Some commercial enterprises invite potential suppliers to register with their online databases in order to be considered for future sourcing opportunities.[4] All online registrants are prequalified before they are invited to participate. The screening process can be similar to that outlined in Chapter Five, in which the intensity of screening depends on the type of purchase. Even if the current supply base has performed well in the past, it is useful to engage in these market research activities to explore new options and ensure that the supply base remains optimal. The extent of this search depends on the sourcing strategy and the cost-benefit trade-off.

The supplier database represents an opportunity for the enterprise to manage and disseminate knowledge across time, staff, units, and transactions. Supplier databases are extremely useful in market research and supplier selection because they are internally maintained and can be updated as frequently as the enterprise determines. However, this is not without cost. There are resources required to maintain accurate supplier information files. To reduce costs while maintaining up-to-date information on suppliers, many commercial enterprises now maintain supplier portals that allow current suppliers to update certain elements of the database, such as contact information, product and specifications, and related information.[5, 6]

The database should include any data collected from the supplier. For former and current suppliers, the database should include information about contracts, such as the terms, products purchased, and expiration date. The most critical element of the database is performance data on current and past contracts. The performance data must be used to determine whether these suppliers should be considered for new sourcing opportunities. Relevant data for supplier information files depend on the product but may include the following:

- supplier contact information—name, address, phone, email, management contact information (e.g., officers and local representatives)
- product and related information—product lines, product specifications, and plant information
- performance—overall, delivery, quality, cost, and other key performance indicators
- prequalifications or certifications—capabilities, quality, and safety (e.g., ISO-9000)
- contract terms—volume, conditions, and start and termination dates.

---

[4]   Some enterprises also use supplier portals to identify diversity suppliers.

[5]   Enterprises allow suppliers limited access to update these data. For example, the suppliers may be allowed to update information about management and representatives as well as update product offerings and other information. Suppliers may also have access to view, but not change, their own performance ratings.

[6]   Supplier portals also allow the enterprise to share relevant information with the supplier, such as demand forecasts and performance ratings. The supplier would be allowed to view his own, but not others', data.

### Supplier Web Sites

Supplier Web sites are a useful source for identifying potential suppliers. The Web sites often provide contact and management information, specific information on product lines and capabilities, and additional information for supplier analysis (e.g., supplier size, production information, and financial reports). Many suppliers now also post annual reports and catalogs on their Web sites.

### Supplier Catalogs

Supplier catalogs are useful sources of information on supplier capabilities and product offerings. Supply managers use these catalogs to identify potential sources of supply as well as to estimate prices and TCOs. Increasingly, these catalogs are available and searchable online at the supplier Web site.

### Supplier Annual Reports

Annual reports contain supplier-specific information on personnel, financial performance, production, and product offerings. Many public suppliers now post their annual reports on their Web sites. While useful, annual reports disclose information about only a point in time and a single supplier. Collecting annual reports over some relevant time period adds additional information about trends in the supplier's performance that may not necessarily be clear in a single report. Annual reports also tend to focus on the overall production or health of a supplier rather than on the performance of particular units or product lines that might interest the buyer. Because these reports are updated only annually, the information may not be as current as necessary.

### Industry Web Sites

Industry associations can offer lists of members who might qualify as potential suppliers, information on industry standards, and information on trade shows and events.

### Trade Registers and Directories

Trade registers and directories, such as ThomasNet.com, Thomas Global Register, and Kompass.com, contain standard contact information for suppliers such as addresses, number of branches, and affiliations. Some information on financial standing may also be useful for supplier evaluation. The registers are indexed by commodity, manufacturer, and trade name or trademark description of the item. There is a cost associated with many of these sources.

### Trade Journals

Suppliers will often advertise their products in trade journals targeted to their intended customers. As a result, trade journals are a useful resource for identifying potential suppliers. Trade journals are industry specific and may vary by commodity. For example, a manufacturer for aerospace parts may advertise in aerospace and engineering journals, such as *Aviation Week*. Journals are now available electronically with search options. In addition to identification of suppliers, trade journals are useful to commodity teams tracking industry trends and benchmarking best practices.

### Trade Associations

Trade associations may sponsor events where buyers and suppliers can meet and also provide information via Web sites and publications. Trade shows are useful means to learn about the industry, meet individual suppliers, learn about new products and modifications, and compare products across suppliers.

### Phone Directories

Online phone directories can be a useful starting point for identifying potential sources for certain types of purchases (e.g., local landscaping firms). However, phone books provide only very basic and limited information, such as the contact and the general industry.

### Supplier Sales Personnel

Supplier sales personnel know their own enterprise, products, and capabilities. Such knowledge allows them to discuss capabilities, offer new applications for their products, and discuss prices and other contract terms.

### Professional Purchasing Organizations and Other Purchasing Professionals

These organizations provide general information about best purchasing practices and highlight examples of exceptional performance. The exchange of information between supply management departments (both colleagues and competitors) provides a useful resource for identifying, evaluating, and benchmarking potential suppliers. Supply management associations, such as the Institute for Supply Management (ISM, formerly NAPM) and the National Institute of Governmental Purchasing, publish membership lists and host educational events to facilitate sharing of information across purchasing professionals. Benchmarking and best practices are also available from purchasing journals.[7]

### Enterprise Personnel (Corporate Knowledge)

The enterprise should exploit the knowledge and experiences of its own personnel within the enterprise. Some of this information is now captured in the supplier database, but formal and informal discussions within the enterprise can also be useful. This type of information is not limited to purchasing professionals. Personnel in other functional areas (e.g., manufacturing and engineering), units, locations, or commodity teams may have useful insights about particular products, suppliers, and practices from their own experiences or through peer interactions.

---

[7]  Purchasing journals, such as *Purchasing,* are also useful resources for procurement personnel. Such journals promote best practices for purchasing, often highlighting a particular industry or commercial firm.

## Summary

### Review: What to Do

1. Identify and make a list of suppliers of the goods and/or services needed.
2. If substitute products are available and workable, include suppliers of these products on the supplier list.

### Where to Look for Relevant Information

Identifying the right suppliers is especially dependent on looking in the right places. The knowledge that the enterprise has gained from its own experiences with suppliers is critical. Managing and utilizing that knowledge should be one of the enterprise's goals. Internal and external sources of industry information are suggested below:

- supplier database
- supplier Web sites
- supplier catalogs
- supplier annual reports
- industry Web sites
- trade registers and directories
- trade journals
- trade associations
- phone directories
- supplier sales personnel
- professional purchasing organizations and other purchasing professionals
- enterprise personnel.

# CHAPTER FIVE

# Evaluate Potential Suppliers

After identification, the next step in market research is to evaluate the potential suppliers of the needed goods or services in order to select the appropriate sources. Detailed data must be collected on individual suppliers, including general information on the supplier and products, financial information, performance, the cost of the good or service, and specific capabilities and capacities. Supplier evaluation—and the data and analyses undertaken to support it—should be tailored to the nature, criticality, and dollar value of the good or service. This chapter provides an outline of an iterative four-stage evaluation process based on Burt, Dobler, and Starling, 2003. Appendixes C and D list some online resources for evaluating suppliers generally and for collecting financial data. Appendix E provides sample templates and forms for supplier evaluations, plant visits, and supplier scorecards.

The industry analysis described in Chapter Three is important in its own right in that it enables the enterprise to understand the realities of the market for a product and develop its sourcing strategy accordingly. But the industry analysis also provides a context for evaluating potential suppliers. For example, it is important to determine whether the industry is financially profitable and then where a potential supplier fits into the industry's financial performance. Market research provides that context. A review of annual reports may reveal that a potential supplier is experiencing lower-than-average and lower-than-expected profits. But how does that supplier's performance compare with those of its competitors and to the industry as a whole? Are there general trends in the industry that explain the supplier's shortfall, such as unexpected shocks to its input prices? Or is the supplier underperforming relative to peers and to the industry as a whole?

Potential suppliers must be evaluated to determine their suitability. Supplier evaluation is an expensive and resource-intensive process that should be tailored to the importance of the purchase. Evaluations for strategic purchases might include all four stages, while less strategic purchases might involve only the earlier stages. Supplier evaluation is also an iterative and sequential process. It would be prohibitive to investigate all potential suppliers thoroughly. While strategic purchases require extensive market research, not all potential suppliers should be investigated extensively. Evaluation should begin with readily available data and data that can be collected with minimal costs. More costly and time-intensive evaluation should be reserved for later stages when the pool of potential suppliers has been narrowed substantially. The team must eliminate suppliers at each stage of the evaluation process to ensure that only qualified suppliers are evaluated at the more costly and time-consuming stages:

- Stage 1: Preliminary analysis
- Stage 2: Financial analysis
- Stage 3: Analyses of performance, costs, and capabilities
- Stage 4: Evaluation conference between the buyer and the supplier.

### Interview Lessons: Looking Beyond First-Tier Suppliers

In theory, supplier evaluation for the most strategic purchases should not be limited to first-tier suppliers but should also extend to lower tiers in the supply chain—the suppliers' suppliers. The enterprise should be able to evaluate second-tier suppliers using the first-tier supplier's data. However, this is ambitious and costly. And suppliers—particularly smaller ones—do not necessarily have the information on hand nor the capability and resources to collect it. As such, reality often limits the enterprise's evaluation to first-tier suppliers. The enterprises we interviewed acknowledged that sharing information with suppliers beyond the first tier was a work in progress. The enterprises had made great inroads in working with first-tier suppliers, but moving beyond the first tier was difficult.

Potential sources for supplier information include internal supplier databases, the suppliers themselves, third-party sources, and primary data collection. The internal supplier database should contain information on current and former suppliers. Supplier Web sites, catalogs, annual reports, and personnel are important sources of information on supplier characteristics, product lines, performance, and capabilities. Third-party sources include trade associations, consultants, auditors, standard-setting organizations, journals, newspapers, local organizations (e.g., the chamber of commerce), state and federal governments, international organizations, the financial community, and regulatory agencies.[1] Other third-party observers include enterprises that sell information about suppliers, such as financial databases and market intelligence sources (e.g., D&B). Primary data collection includes requests for qualifications, requests for information (or information sheets), test data, site visits to suppliers, and interviews with supplier staff. When warranted by the importance of the purchase, primary data collection should be used to supplement the published resources. Less expensive methods include requests for information and requests for qualifications. More expensive methods include site visits and interviews. The method should be tailored to the importance of the purchase.

## Stage 1: Preliminary Analysis

The first step is to review general information on both the supplier and the product. This preliminary analysis should include a basic evaluation of the following elements:

---

[1]   Some third-party data are available free of charge, while others may be available only with a subscription or purchase cost.

> **Interview Lessons: Prequalified Suppliers**
>
> The benefits of market research lie in knowledge management. Ongoing market research enables the enterprise to have the information on hand when needed. Documented supplier selection and evaluation processes, as well as a centralized supplier database, ensure that the information is passed from one transaction to the next—thus avoiding a repetition of costs. Often, enterprises used their market research to prequalify a list of suppliers. These suppliers have been qualified in key aspects—such as cost, quality, delivery, or safety. Their prequalified status allowed the enterprise to make a contract award quickly when demand is generated. Some commercial enterprises qualified potential suppliers when they register online, though the extent of the qualification process depends on the type of supplier and purchase.

- Management: officers and titles, education, experience
- Finance: bank and credit references
- References: list of customers (or past performance if current or former supplier)
- Size: annual sales or revenue, number of employees, space occupied
- Trends: annual history of sales, revenues, production
- Future plans: plant openings, new locations
- Other issues: certifications (e.g., ISO-9000).

Ideally, much of this information should already be available in the internal supplier database for current, former, and prequalified suppliers. For suppliers not already in the enterprise's database, these data may be available from existing sources, such as supplier Web sites, supplier annual reports, and third-party sources, or they can be collected from the supplier using a general information sheet (i.e., a preliminary request for information).

A supplier should be eliminated if the supplier or the product does not satisfy requirements or the data indicate that the supplier represents a significant risk. The team should retain only suppliers who are capable of providing the right product at a required quantity and quality. For example, suppliers who lack sufficient financial or performance credentials (e.g., references) or who failed to perform satisfactorily on key performance indicators in previous contracts can be eliminated. Likewise, potential suppliers who do not meet required certifications (e.g., ISO-9000) or who are too small or too large may also be eliminated.[2]

---

[2]  See Chapter Two and Appendix B for issues regarding supplier size.

## Stage 2: Financial Analysis

For potential suppliers who have survived the initial evaluation, information should be collected to assess financial stability. Financial stability is critical because it ensures that the supplier can meet delivery requirements, respond to changes, and meet other demands, such as sustained support of the product. Support is important for certain types of purchases, e.g., aircraft engines and construction. Financially unstable suppliers may not be able to provide long-term support, either because of financial hardship or because of exit from the industry (e.g., due to bankruptcy, sale, or financial motivations).

Financial measures of particular interest in evaluating the financial stability and health of suppliers focus on liquidity, turnover, profitability, and debt. Some measures are interpretable on their own, while others require market research on industry norms (or averages) for interpretation. Industry norms for some measures are available from *Annual Statement Studies* by Risk Management Association (RMA) or from D&B's *Industry Norms and Key Business Ratios*. Financial performance is measured by liquidity measures, funds management ratios, profitability measures, and measures of long-term financial strength. We list sample measures in Table 5.1. Table D.2, in Appendix D, provides a more detailed list of measures, definitions, calculations, and interpretations of the financial measures.

Financial performance serves as a critical indicator of whether to include or exclude potential suppliers. Financially unstable suppliers should be eliminated from the pool of potential suppliers because they represent a risk to the enterprise. They may fail to deliver products on time or require the enterprise to assist them financially (or otherwise) to ensure delivery. Risky suppliers should be eliminated from the supply base at this stage before additional resources are dedicated to the more intensive and expensive performance, cost, and capability analyses.

**Table 5.1**
**Sample Financial Indicators**

| Type of Measure | Potential Indicators |
| --- | --- |
| Liquidity | Working capital<br>Current ratio<br>Quick ratio |
| Funds management | Ratio of receivables to sales<br>Average collection period<br>Average accounts payable period<br>Inventory turnover<br>Average days in inventory<br>Fixed asset turnover |
| Profitability | Profit margin<br>Gross profit margin<br>Return on assets<br>Return on equity |
| Long-term financial strength | Debt-to-equity ratio<br>times interest earned |

SOURCE: Burt, Dobler, and Starling, 2003, pp. 355ff. *World Class Supply Management: The Key to Supply Chain Management,* 7th ed., © The McGraw-Hill Companies, Inc., 2003. Used by permission.
NOTE: See Table D.2, in Appendix D, for definitions of terms.

Financial data are available from a variety of existing sources, such as income statements and balance sheets in annual reports. Income statements provide information regarding earnings, net income, net sales, gross profit, contribution margins, and cost structures.[3] The balance sheet summarizes the supplier's financial position at a point in time with respect to assets and liabilities. The balance sheet shows the age of accounts payable and receivable, inventory status, cash, and remaining accounting life of capital equipment. Trends or changes in the income statements can be used to identify rising costs, declining profits, or declining sales, but such an analysis requires accumulating years of data (perhaps from sequential annual reports). Data may be more readily available for publicly owned enterprises; however, some information is also available for private enterprises. Financial data can be collected either from existing sources or directly from the supplier as a condition of his eligibility for award of the purchase. Financial indicators should be compared across suppliers and with the industry averages in terms of both their current levels and changes over time. An analysis of trends in supplier financials may warn of forthcoming problems if there is a deterioration of performance. Potential sources for this information include suppliers, D&B reports, annual reports, Moody's Industrials, RMA, and third-party evaluators and observers (e.g., *Inc.* 500). Table D.1, in Appendix D, lists online sources for financial data.

## Stage 3: Analyses of Performance, Cost, and Capabilities

Much of the analysis thus far has utilized less costly data available from existing sources or collected remotely from the supplier. Such analyses may be sufficient for many purchases. But for more important purchases, these data may be used to narrow the potential pool of suppliers before more resource-intensive evaluation. The next steps are to assess performance, cost, and capabilities. The data necessary in this stage are often more difficult and costly to obtain. Internal supplier databases can be a critical resource to assess supplier performance, cost, and capabilities—especially for current and former suppliers. However, some additional data may have to be collected from the supplier. A first pass at this information may be obtained using a request for information. Requests for information are less expensive and less time-consuming than site visits to a large number of suppliers. Requests for information and first-hand determination of supplier capabilities (i.e., site visits and interviews) are used to evaluate supplier capabilities along a number of factors. However, strategic purchases may require more-intensive evaluation and first-hand analysis of specific capabilities via facility visits. This process is costly for both the buyer and the suppliers in terms of resources—particularly personnel time—and thus must be reserved for high-value strategic goods and services and for likely suppliers.

### Performance Analyses

How has the supplier performed on previous purchases with respect to the enterprise's expectations overall and with respect to individual metrics (e.g., cost, quality, and delivery)? The

---

[3]  Income statements are enterprise-wide. As a result, the cost structure from an income statement is most informative for single-product enterprises.

enterprise should take advantage of its first-hand experiences with suppliers by tracking and considering past performance. This performance assessment can include many characteristics, but it should be consistent with the enterprise's strategic goals. For example, the enterprise may track supplier performance with respect to quality, schedule, and cost. A database with supplier performance history is a useful evaluation tool because it allows experiences to be passed to personnel not directly involved in previous purchases.

Although the enterprise does not have direct experience with suppliers not currently or formerly in its supply base, it is important to conduct similar analyses for these suppliers. With respect to performance, the enterprise must rely on reputation, primary data collection, and personal interaction rather than prior experience. For example, the enterprise may request reference letters from other enterprises with which the supplier does business, collect test samples and data, or personnel may visit the supplier in person. The information on supplier performance is complemented by the industry analysis. Enterprise performance should be put in the context of the industry. For example, quality performance on key metrics, such as defect rate, should be assessed against the performance of competitors and benchmarks for the industry.

---

**Interview Lessons: Performance Data**

Supplier databases are a tool for knowledge management*—they reduce the time and effort necessary to source and renew contracts. The databases are a useful resource for the decision to continue, increase, or discontinue business with a supplier. They are also useful for finding suppliers for new contracts. For example, the database contains capabilities data, which summarize the products made by the supplier. In searching for a supplier for a new contract, the enterprise can search its current suppliers in good standing who provide the necessary good or service.** This approach builds on previous efforts to rationalize and optimize the supply base. Source selection and supplier management processes are data driven, and substantial information for supplier selection should be available and managed in-house. The supplier database includes performance data, products, capabilities, capacity, management information, contacts, contract details, location, quality certifications, internal prequalifications, financial information, and other factors. Performance data are key. Performance measures track key indexes, such as quality, cost, and delivery as well as overall scores based on all measures. Performance measures and ratings are well-defined to ensure consistency. As one enterprise noted, simply tracking performance is not sufficient. These data must be used to make future sourcing decisions in order to incentivize supplier performance.

* Knowledge management is the deliberate effort to maximize an organization's performance through creating, sharing, and leveraging knowledge and experience from internal and external sources (Upstream CIO, http://www.upstreamcio.com/glossary.asp, as of March 2006).

** This process does not preclude the enterprise from evaluating new suppliers.

**Interview Lessons: Scorecards for Potential Suppliers***

If the enterprise maintains records of supplier performance, it is at an advantage when evaluating a current or former supplier. The enterprise does not have comparable data for new potential suppliers. One enterprise developed evaluation scorecards for the site visits that allowed the site visit team to rate the prospective supplier based on criteria similar to the performance metrics collected for current suppliers. The information gathered touched on the same performance areas as the current supplier performance database because these metrics were aligned with the enterprise's strategic and supply objectives.

* Appendix E provides an example of an evaluation scorecard.

## Cost Analyses

During the industry analysis, the team should have developed an understanding of the key cost drivers within an industry. In essence, the team now has a general understanding of what the product *should* cost and the TCO. During this phase of the supplier evaluation process, individual suppliers should be assessed within that context. Understanding the cost structure of suppliers is an important element in evaluating the supplier's efficiency as well as in identifying areas for improvement. The should-cost and TCO analyses for each supplier parallel the industry analyses described in Chapter Three, but they are calculated for individual suppliers for comparison purposes.

To evaluate the purchase price, the buyer must understand the supplier's costs, including direct labor costs, indirect labor costs, material costs, manufacturing or process operating costs, and general overhead costs. The commodity team must have developed a clear understanding of the market and the ability to evaluate how changes in upstream markets or inputs may affect costs. Supplier costs may differ substantially across suppliers as a result of differences in production processes, input prices, cost advantages, economies of scale, economies of scope, and a number of other factors. The industry analyses in Chapter Three should provide some insight into these issues. But specific cost information on individual suppliers may be difficult to gather, in part because some suppliers do not track their costs in much detail and partly because the suppliers prefer not to share potentially sensitive cost data. Some suppliers will instead offer approximations. The sharing of cost data often requires a high level of trust and commitment. For some purchases, the enterprise may require that the potential suppliers share their cost data.

For the TCO analysis, the commodity team must have a thorough understanding of all the costs (to the buyer) associated with the purchase. These include costs incurred before, during, and after the transaction. TCO analyses of individual suppliers may reveal that the low-priced supplier is not always the lowest-cost or best-value supplier. For example, the low-price supplier may be located farther away, forcing the buyer to incur higher costs for shipping. Or the low-price supplier may have a higher defect rate or more delivery failures, which will increase the incidence of line stoppages and consequently the costs to the enterprise. Chapter Three provides a full description of TCO for the industry analyses, but the same approach can be applied to individual suppliers.[4]

The cost analyses described in this section rely on supplier cost information. Enterprises now request cost data from their suppliers. It should be clear whether the supplier has the ability to track his own costs in a method that is consistent with industry standards, such as activity-based costing.[5] Activity-based costing ensures that the supplier is able to segregate costs (including proper allocation of overhead costs) by task. This ability ensures that the supplier understands his own processes and also indicates that the supplier can share relevant cost information with the enterprise. Such information is critical to the supplier and enterprise working together to produce continuous improvements in costs.

## Capability Analyses

The capabilities of suppliers must be analyzed along all criteria relevant to the purchase, subject to the criticality of the purchase. We have already discussed prices and costs. However, lowest price or even lowest cost is not the only—and often not the most important—criteria along which suppliers should be evaluated. The lowest-price bidder or even the supplier with the lowest total cost is not the *best value* supplier if he cannot deliver the product with the correct requirements, specifications, quality, and schedule. In evaluating these criteria, it is important to remember that the supplier must meet the needs of the buyer. Primary areas for capability analyses include quality, service (e.g., delivery), and capacity. Other areas evaluated as required by the purchase include engineering, flexibility, management, information technology, and distribution.

Site visits to evaluate particular capabilities should have specific goals in order to be effective. The capabilities to be assessed and the criticality of the purchase will determine the makeup of the site visit team. The makeup of the site visit team may also depend on whether the product is in the design phase or a product already in production. Table 5.2 lists the common elements of capability analyses (based on Monczka, Trent, and Handfield, 2001; Burt, Dobler, and Starling, 2003): quality, service, capacity, engineering, distribution, flexibility, management, and information technology.

**Quality capabilities** of the supplier are integral to the quality of the purchasing enterprise's own end product. Quality capability analyses examine the ability of the supplier to deliver the product with the appropriate level of quality. The analyses should address the technical ability of the supplier to deliver the product with the appropriate specifications. The quality of the product can be measured via defect rates and mean time between failures based on samples, test data, and (where possible) past performance. Many enterprises track the quality of inputs purchased from individual suppliers in an effort to implement continuous improvement and to trace the cause of their own production, quality, and customer satisfaction problems (e.g., job

---

[4]  Further details on TCO can be found in Burt, Dobler, and Starling, 2003; and Monczka, Trent, and Handfield, 2001. As noted in Chapter Three, a related technique is ZBP (see Burt, Norquist, and Anklesaria, 1990).

[5]  The supplier's accounting practices should also be consistent with generally accepted accounting principles.

**Table 5.2**
**Areas for Capability Analyses**

| Capability Factors | Sample Issues |
| --- | --- |
| Quality capability | Technical ability to meet required specifications<br>Quality history (e.g., mean time between failures, defect rates, warranty issues, test data, and returns)<br>Process quality (e.g., ISO-9000 certification)<br>Attitude toward quality (e.g., total quality management)<br>Design of experiments |
| Service capability | Delivery (e.g., late, early, and incomplete deliveries; lead time; regular orders; special orders; and back orders)<br>Other delivery/schedule issues (e.g., dispute settlement and advance notice of price changes or shortages)<br>Post-sale service (e.g., warranties and after-market support) |
| Capacity capability | Supplier capacity (e.g., potential output)<br>Supplier volume (e.g., actual output and sales)<br>Available capacity (e.g., ratio of capacity to volume)<br>Excess capacity (e.g., layoffs, plant closings, and idle machinery)<br>Excess demand (e.g., extra shifts, overtime, and temporary labor) |
| Engineering capability | Innovation<br>Safety (in design and production)<br>Overspecification |
| Flexibility capability (JIT) | Capacity to adjust production on short notice<br>Lean systems<br>Trained staff equipped to implement JIT systems<br>High degree of integration between the enterprise and the supplier (e.g., single-source collaborative relationships) |
| Management capability | Good management evident at all levels of the enterprise (e.g., well-trained staff and absence of labor issues)<br>Management style, attitude, and compatibility |
| Information technology capability | Ability to share information between supplier and enterprise |
| Distribution capability | Access to distribution<br>Ownership of distribution assets (e.g., facilities and vehicles) |

SOURCE: Adapted from Burt, Dobler, and Starling, 2003, pp. 334ff.

stops, defects, and time to failure) with the end product. Process quality is also an important factor. With respect to quality and engineering capability, the enterprise may conduct its own evaluation for critical purchases or it may rely on external information, including references and third-party certification (e.g., ISO-9000). Finally, the commitment or attitude of the supplier toward quality can be assessed by the existence of a total quality management (TQM) process or other quality controls. TQM implies that four critical components of quality are present within the supplier (see Raedels, 2000, p. 161): (1) a commitment to quality among top management, (2) an emphasis on employee education and training, (3) statistical methods to ensure quality, and (4) collection and analysis of customer feedback to improve operations and processes.

**Service capabilities** measure a variety of factors. Delivery is the most commonly measured element of service. The supplier must be able to deliver the order at the requested time;

early deliveries, late deliveries, and incomplete shipments are indicators of negative performance. Late and incomplete shipments interfere with production, while early shipments create inventory costs. More-detailed delivery metrics may track lead time, back orders, and responsiveness to special orders. But service measures extend beyond delivery. Other service metrics include advanced notice (e.g., for price changes or for incomplete deliveries) and post-sales services, such as warranties and after-market support.

**Capacity capability** analyses examine the ability of the supplier to deliver the quantities required by the buyer. Capacity measures potential production (i.e., output) and is a measure of supplier size. Volume measures, including actual sales and production output, are often used as a proxy for capacity, but capacity actually encompasses what the supplier can produce rather than actual production; so it is necessary to assess available capacity—the potential output not already in production. Indicators for excess capacity include plant closings, layoffs, and idle machinery, whereas overtime and extra shifts suggest that the supplier may be overcommitted.[6] The commodity team must ensure that the supplier is sufficiently large to ensure that the supplier can deliver the required product and to avoid dependence on the part of the supplier. A rule of thumb is that the purchase should not be more than 15 to 25 percent of the supplier's capacity (Burt, Dobler, and Starling, 2003). But it is important to keep in mind that the required capacity must be available (i.e., not committed to other buyers).

Cost, quality, and delivery are by far the most common areas for assessment and measurement. However, certain types of purchases may require additional analyses. For some technical purchases, it may be necessary to evaluate the supplier's **engineering capabilities,** including ability to innovate, attention to safety concerns in design and production, design of experiments, and knowledge in matching product specifications to the needs of the buyer. For buyers

---

**Interview Lessons: Supplier Attitude**

The enterprises interviewed for this study cited supplier attitude as critical. Suppliers who were not willing to meet expectations and to work closely with the enterprise were not considered for future sourcing. Supplier attitude cannot be regulated. Both parties must be willing to enter a particular type of relationship by taking the time and making the commitment to develop personal relationships and trust. In ongoing relationships, supplier attitude is reflected in past performance and responsiveness to the enterprise's needs and can be measured through surveys. For suppliers with whom the enterprise has no previous experience, site visits to initiate personal contact are useful. Of course, the attitude of the enterprise is also important. Purchasing enterprises should consider suppliers as partners to ensure mutual benefits. The enterprise must work with the supplier to achieve the required goals by sharing necessary information, providing feedback, and other activities (e.g., supplier conferences).

---

[6]  Capacity is a function of size and as such should be matched to the needs of the buyer—an issue that is discussed further in Appendix B. For example, the supplier must have sufficient available capacity to meet the buyer's demand. However, the most appropriate supplier may not be the largest supplier if the buyer's purchase volume is simply too small to generate enough interest on the part of a larger supplier.

interested in JIT systems, it is important to conduct an analysis of the supplier's capabilities in this regard—particularly his **flexibility capabilities** to assess the supplier's ability to adjust production to meet unexpected demand changes. Other evidence includes lean systems, staff training in JIT systems, and existing JIT relationships with other buyers.[7] **Management capability** examines how well the supplier is organized and operated. Evidence includes good supplier performance, well-trained personnel, and good internal labor relations (e.g., no strikes and no contractual disputes).[8] The management style of the supplier must also be compatible with that of the enterprise; this is a more subjective measure that can be evaluated via site visits. The **information technology capabilities** of the supplier must be capable of meeting the needs of the buyer. For example, is the supplier able to share and receive the necessary information with the buyer? Finally, in some cases, it may be necessary to evaluate the supplier's **distribution capabilities,** including access to distribution or ownership of distribution capabilities to deliver the product to the buyer.

## Stage 4: Evaluation Conference Between the Buyer and the Supplier

Extremely critical purchases may require an evaluation conference—a meeting between enterprise management and supplier representatives—to finalize selection. This is an opportunity for management to visit the supplier's plant to discuss any critical issues associated with the purchase. This meeting is useful to evaluate the supplier's understanding of the complexity and/or criticality of the purchase.

## Summary

### Review: What to Do

Potential suppliers must be evaluated to determine their suitability. The evaluation process is an iterative process that eliminates unsuitable suppliers early. Only qualified suppliers advance to later stages of the market research process, which require the commitment of more resources and effort.

1. Collect basic data on potential suppliers. Eliminate unqualified suppliers.
2. Conduct financial evaluation of suppliers. Eliminate financially unstable suppliers.
3. Analyze the suppliers' capabilities. Eliminate suppliers who do not meet requirements.
   a. Evaluate performance data.
      - Use past performance data for suppliers currently or formerly in the supply base.
      - Use third-party data, supplier data, or potential supplier scorecards for new suppliers.
   b. Analyze cost, quality, service, and capacity.

---

[7]   Some leading commercial enterprises offer JIT training for key suppliers.

[8]   Financial performance may also indicate sound management, but financial performance should have already been evaluated in the second stage of the evaluation.

    c.   Analyze other capabilities as required by the individual purchase.
4.   Conduct an evaluation conference between management of both the enterprise and the supplier, if necessary.

**Where to Look for Relevant Information**

The following sources of information will be helpful in conducting the analyses described in this chapter:

- internal supplier database
- supplier Web sites
- third-party observers
- primary data collection.

# CHAPTER SIX

# Manage the Supply Base[1]

It is important to keep in mind that the benefits of market research and supplier evaluation are not limited to source selection. Industry and supplier information relating to costs, quality, delivery, and other capabilities also strengthen the negotiating position of the enterprise on contract terms and performance expectations.

Market research clearly plays a role in understanding the industry, selecting a source, and negotiating the terms of the purchase.[2] But market research does not end when the contract is signed. Rather, it continues to inform the management of existing supplier relationships and development of new relationships when necessary. Commodity teams should monitor suppliers and the industry on an ongoing basis to ensure that the supply base and practices remain optimal. Tracking the performance of current suppliers is a key element of supply base management. With respect to the industry, commodity teams should remain aware of changing market conditions, technological changes, costs, capacity, quality, and other outcomes of interest to the enterprise.[3] A second way in which market research can help manage the supply base is the identification of opportunities for supplier development.

## Monitor Suppliers and the Industry

The enterprise should monitor and evaluate suppliers on a periodic basis to ensure that they continue to represent the best suppliers for the enterprise. This process is most useful in conjunction with monitoring of the industry itself. Changes in the industry may reveal a need to reevaluate the choice of suppliers and/or practices. Industries may expand to include new suppliers as technology adoption progresses or as restrictions (e.g., patents) are eased. Alternatively, the suppliers in an industry may remain the same, but the emergence of new technology shifts the industry structure. The team should be aware of trends—such as shifts in supplier input prices, scarcity of materials, and changes in labor markets—that may affect sourcing. Awareness of changes in product characteristics—such as quality, technology, safety, and reli-

---

[1]  This chapter is based on Burt, Dobler, and Starling, 2003; and Raedels, 2000.

[2]  Although not discussed in this document, it should be clear that the price, TCO, benchmarks, and other data can be useful in negotiating terms with suppliers.

[3]  This is akin to the Air Force's market surveillance.

ability—is also critical to retaining an optimal supply base. For example, have the current suppliers adopted new processes that improve quality?

Performance metrics for monitoring supplier performance vary by industry. The most commonly monitored performance indicators measure quality, service (e.g., delivery), and cost with specific measures and targets tailored to the product and industry ("Quality Designated as Most Essential Supplier Performance Metric," 1999). For some industries, innovation and other factors may also be tracked. Performance measures must be constructed carefully to reflect the areas of interest to the buyer. Enterprises indicate that you get what you measure; so performance metrics must be aligned with the enterprise's goals and objectives. There are often multiple measures for each category. Delivery measures can account for late and early shipments, partial deliveries, improper labeling, and other factors. These individual metrics are weighted to yield an overall score for the performance area (e.g., delivery). Performance metrics across categories (e.g., quality, delivery, and cost) are also weighted to create an overall performance score for each supplier. In aggregating the metrics, the enterprise must ensure that the weighting of factors accurately reflects the importance of each factor.

Regular reports focus the attention of suppliers' management on performance. Monthly or quarterly reports that update individual suppliers on their own performance can be a useful mechanism for relaying information and tracking progress toward goals. The metrics must be populated carefully. Inaccurate data, improper weighting of factors, and use of subjective measures can undermine performance measurement systems and their ability to bring about change. The enterprise must support performance measures by creating a process that ensures data quality. Data quality requires a system that accurately tracks performance and allows suppliers to dispute the numbers by creating an appeals process. A supplier's own ratings information should be shared with the supplier, but not with his competitors. In some cases, it may also be useful to share anonymous rankings of suppliers to educate the supplier on its performance relative to its competitors.

The supplier's reaction to ratings will also depend on how they are presented. Ratings should be presented in a constructive and problem-solving manner to identify opportunities for improvement. Joint efforts to help the supplier improve performance are an integral part of supplier development programs. While poor performance initiates a problem-solving approach, the supplier must show some improvement within a few months. If there is no improvement, the supplier will eventually be dropped from the supply base. Although the ratings should be used in a constructive manner to bring about improvement, the ratings must also play a critical role in source selection in order to incentivize suppliers. Enterprises use performance ratings to determine which suppliers should receive more, the same, or less business in the future in order to recognize (and encourage) superior performance. Comparisons should also be made to information gathered in market research to determine whether the enterprise should shift to a new supplier.

This monitoring process is especially useful for monitoring performance of key supplier relationships. These suppliers may comprise a significant share of spend, offer a critical input, be the sole or single source, or offer a differentiated product that makes switching difficult and/ or costly. In theses cases, because switching to another supplier would be difficult or impossible, it is important to maintain a good relationship and an understanding of how the supplier is performing relative to alternatives. Ongoing monitoring may highlight problems before they become critical and offer opportunities for improvement. For these suppliers, monitoring may be more intensive than the typical performance metrics. The commodity team may also track a supplier's strategic plans. Does the supplier have plans to expand in terms of production capacity? Are there plans to increase capabilities for new products or processes? How would these changes affect the enterprise?

## Developing Suppliers

Market research can also direct supplier development efforts—these are activities undertaken by the enterprise to improve supplier performance (Burt, Dobler, and Starling, 2003). Supplier development efforts can be directed toward the current supply base or toward a new supplier.

Market research and monitoring of supplier performance can identify areas for improvement in the supply base. Supplier development for existing suppliers can focus on addressing shortfalls in performance for particular suppliers. For example, the enterprise may dispatch a team to help a troubled supplier with cost-control problems. In other cases, the enterprise may assist an existing supplier in developing the technical expertise to supply a new product or meet more-stringent specifications. Alternatively, supplier development may be more general. This might include training for supplier personnel in Six Sigma or lean processes (e.g., JIT) as well as the formation of joint teams (e.g., engineering) to develop improvements that benefit both the supplier and the enterprise. The level of developmental support offered to existing suppliers depends on their importance. For example, the enterprise may offer on-site training to key suppliers, but online training to less important suppliers.

But development activities can also focus on potential suppliers. For example, what if market research reveals that the right supplier does not exist? In this case, the enterprise may have to invest some resources in developing the appropriate supplier. The assistance may simply involve training the new supplier to be more cost-effective or to meet more stringent product specifications. This approach is resource intensive and should be undertaken only if existing suppliers fail to address the enterprise's needs.

### Interview Lessons: Supplier Development

If market research indicates that suppliers are unable to meet the requirements of the enterprise, supplier development may be necessary. At one enterprise, interviewees noted that they invested substantial resources in supplier development. They believed that their own success was inherently linked to the health and success of their suppliers. One executive we interviewed noted that his enterprise could not be low cost if its suppliers were not low cost. Rather than simply requiring that suppliers lower prices, the enterprise invested resources in training its suppliers.

## Summary

### Review: What to Do

Market research does not end with source selection. The commodity team should continue to monitor current suppliers and the industry to ensure that the supply base remains optimal. Supplier development activities can address performance shortcomings and gaps in available supply:

1. Monitor the market to ensure that the supply base and practices remain optimal.
2. Track supplier performance. Communicate ratings and expectations to suppliers.
3. Engage in supplier development activities as necessary and warranted by a cost-benefit analysis.

### Where to Look for Relevant Information

The commodity team must evaluate its internal supplier database—particularly performance of the supply base—against the market and its own needs. Data can be drawn from

- an internal supplier database
- industry and supplier analysis (as outlined in Chapters Three through Five).

# CHAPTER SEVEN

# Putting It All Together: Current Air Force Market Research and Next Steps

As we have discussed throughout this monograph, market research is an important tool to support the Air Force's objectives through improved procurement. The Air Force has in place market research components that are consistent with the recommendations in this monograph. In this chapter, we discuss the Air Force's efforts to date and discuss some lessons from commercial enterprises on moving forward.

## Current Air Force Market Research

The Air Force has three major approaches to promoting the use of market research practices: training, online resources, and the use of consultants. First, the Air Force provides training in market research in two primary locations: the Defense Acquisition University (DAU) at Fort Belvoir (see http://www.dau.mil) and at bases with Acquisition Excellence Directorates (e.g., Warner Robins Air Logistics Center—see http://www.robins.af.mil). DAU offers a two-day course dedicated to market research. Warner Robins has been a driving force for market research training and implementation.[1] Warner Robins has developed formalized processes and training for market research. Warner Robins offers a one-time, two-hour workshop to provide JIT training for existing personnel who are tasked with procurement and general training for new personnel.

Second, the Air Force has developed how-to guides and made these resources available online. Of particular interest are *SD-2*, *SD-5*, and *AFMC Commercial Acquisition Guide*. U.S. Department of Defense, 1996, addresses the purchase of commercial and nondevelopment items. U.S. Department of Defense, 1997, outlines the basic principles of market research, emphasizes the importance of market research at each stage of the acquisition process, and highlights the data requirements to support market research. Air Force Materiel Command, 1998, promotes the use of teams in the sourcing process. Specific segments within the Air Force have also developed further content. For example, Warner Robins personnel developed

---

[1]   In addition, Warner Robins supports Air Force commodity councils.

the "Market Research PoST,"[2] which hosts documents on acquisition and market research policy, market research tools and templates, and sample market research. This Web site also provides links to additional useful information, such as search engines, journal articles, small business portals, and sources for best practices.

Finally, some Air Force locations, such as Warner Robins, have engaged IBM consultants to support commodity councils. IBM developed prototype templates for the Air Force's top five suppliers. More recently, the Air Force engaged Bearing Point for logistics education, instruction, and strategic consulting services.

## Recommendations for the Air Force

Implementation of the market research process outlined in this monograph requires support from the Air Force. The overriding lessons from the literature and interviews with commercial enterprises are relevant to the Air Force's success: (1) improve data availability, quality, and utilization; (2) provide training for commodity teams; and (3) ensure management support and staff buy in.

### Improve Data Availability, Quality, and Utilization

One interviewee at a commercial enterprise noted that "what gets measured gets results." Commercial enterprises collected data on their spend and supplier performance. The Air Force must understand its spend in order to focus and leverage its market research efforts. The Air Force must also track supplier performance. Data collection is key but not sufficient. The data must be easily accessible to relevant stakeholders and be utilized in decisionmaking. Commercial enterprises rely on such data to determine whether existing suppliers should be awarded new projects.

Commodity teams must understand spending on their group of goods and services as well as spending with their primary suppliers. Spending must be tracked accurately and completely to ensure that the enterprise is aware of all of its interactions with each supplier. Commercial enterprises are careful to leverage their total spend through supply base rationalization and consolidation of contracts. One enterprise had recently transformed its purchasing processes, but the start of that transformation was postponed until the enterprise had implemented software to track spend. After the software had been in place for a year, personnel at the enterprise felt they had sufficient information to begin the transformation. Other enterprises used interim data (e.g., from suppliers subject to audit) to start their PSCM efforts until expenditure tracking was in place. The Air Force can use the CBIS and related supplier datasets as an existing source.

Source selection is an intensely data-driven process. The commercial enterprises we interviewed collected extensive data on their experiences with suppliers in order to assess their current performance as well as evaluate their potential for future sourcing. Enterprises create

---

2    This Web site is also called "MR PoST." Some Web site content has been developed in conjunction with IBM consultants.

performance ratings for their suppliers to track quality, cost, delivery, and other relevant factors. Performance on individual criteria and overall performance were important factors in the enterprise's decision to retain a supplier, award new projects to the existing supplier (rather than seek a new source), and improve supplier performance.

## Provide Training for Commodity Teams

Market research requires data collection and analyses beyond traditional Air Force procedures. Collecting and analyzing data in the market research process require well-trained and committed personnel. Market research and analysis must be conducted by teams that are knowledgeable about the industry and comfortable with the techniques necessary to evaluate suppliers. The teams must also be committed to the new approach; as one interviewee stated, "You are on the train or you're at the station." Training must focus on developing these capabilities in-house.

Good market research requires personnel who possess analytic skills and are trained in market research techniques. Documentation and guidelines assist personnel in translating goals into actions. Some commercial enterprises formalize their market research processes to improve knowledge management. Likewise, training programs play an integral part in preparing procurement personnel for the challenges of implementing strategic sourcing. Commercial enterprises invest considerable resources in training and retaining procurement personnel (Ausink, Baldwin, and Paul, 2004). One commercial enterprise we interviewed strongly encouraged its personnel to pursue related degrees (e.g., certified purchasing manager).

While the Air Force's training at DAU and Warner Robins constitutes progress, limited one-time training is unlikely to promote the depth of research and analytic skills necessary to support commodity councils. The commodity councils have the support of consultants, but it is important that the Air Force develop the skills *internally*. Commercial enterprises stressed that consultants were used only on a limited basis, if at all.

## Ensure Management Support and Staff Buy In

Successful implementation of new procurement practices cannot be accomplished without the support of top management and the buy in of relevant personnel. Top Air Force management, like their commercial counterparts, must show continued support for market research and other PSCM efforts. Commercial enterprises made executives responsible for progress and required reporting of progress. Linking enterprise-wide objectives to individual employees and tracking their progress are effective methods for sharing goals and expectations throughout the enterprise and motivating buy in. Tangible successes, such as cost-savings and improved service and quality, can be a motivating force in continued improvements. One interviewee cautioned that buy in is a concern not only at the beginning stages of implementation, but also throughout the process. Enterprises often experience a stumbling block around the two- or three-year mark of their PSCM implementation. There must be steady forward progress and support to ensure that the process does not stall or reverse.

# Interview Protocol

The following interview protocol was used to guide the discussion in interviews with procurement personnel at commercial enterprises.

## Interview Protocol

RAND will observe strict confidentiality with the information we receive; we will not disclose to our sponsor or others the names of individuals or companies participating in this study.

### A. Overall Strategy

1. What is your overall organizational strategy? (e.g., low cost, innovation, high quality)
2. What is the main sourcing strategy used at your firm?
   a. Does your firm segment spend?
   b. If yes, what criteria are used to segment spend? (e.g., Pareto, etc.)
3. To what extent does supply market research play a role in supply strategy development and source selection for your organization?
4. What are the goals of your supply market research?
5. How do you ensure that your supply market research and sourcing strategy remain consistent with the overall organizational strategy?
   a. Who is responsible for forming the organizational and sourcing strategies?
   b. Who is responsible for overseeing market research?
6. What are the most important factors in evaluating internal requirements? (e.g., volume demanded, quality requirements, price, strategic importance)
7. What are the most important characteristics of your products? (e.g., total spend, strategic importance, substitutes, standardization, quality)
8. What are the most important supplier characteristics? (e.g., price, quality, capacity, reputation, past performance, financial stability)
9. What are the most important factors in evaluating your supply market? (e.g., number of suppliers, market concentration, product differentiation, capacity, price variation, innovation)
10. To what extent do you consider the current and future supply markets relative to your needs?

11. Does your firm engage in more-proactive supplier identification and development? (e.g., reverse marketing) When?
12. Have your supply market research processes and practices changed recently?
    a. If yes, how and why have they changed? Please discuss the implementation of these changes.

## B.   Overall Process

1. Do you have formal processes and guidelines for supply market research?
   a. For which segments?
   b. Are these documented?
   c. Are organizational and sourcing strategies also documented?
   d. May we have copies of these documents?
2. How do you support your supply market research processes?
   a. Please describe recruitment, education, and training.
3. What criteria are used to determine the depth and breadth of supply market research? (e.g., spend, strategic importance, new product versus existing product, cost of market research)
4. Who decides how much supply market research is necessary?
   a. When is this decision made?
   b. Does this vary by segment?
5. Describe the typical supply market research process (for each segment, if applicable).
6. Which personnel are involved in supply market research (e.g., procurement, engineers, etc.) at each stage?
   a. Is there any particularly useful functional expertise or background?
7. Do you use teams for supply market research?
   a. If yes, how are teams formed?
   b. Are they permanent commodity councils or temporary cross-functional teams?
   c. What are the relationships (if any) between commodity councils, cross-functional teams, and market research teams?
8. Do you use outside expertise or consultants? If yes, when and why?

## C.   Data Requirements

1. How would you characterize your supply market research?
   a. For example, is it data driven?
2. To what extent does your supply market research rely on existing internal and external information? (e.g., trade journals, D&B financials, third-party evaluations, internal performance assessments)
   a. Describe these data and sources.
3. How much primary data collection efforts are involved in terms of personnel, dollars, etc.?

4.  What form does this data collection take? (e.g., electronic, survey, site visits) At which stage?
5.  Which information resources are most important at each stage of the evaluation?

### D.   Steps in Supply Market Research Process

#### *Supplier Identification*

1.  What are the main resources your enterprise uses for identifying the pool of potential suppliers?
    a.  How have these resources developed/changed recently? (e.g., online)
    b.  Do these resources vary by segment? Or by industry? If yes, how?
2.  How many potential suppliers are typically included in your evaluation process?
    a.  In the initial round? In subsequent rounds?
    b.  How does this vary for each segment? For each industry?
3.  What process or models do you use to determine the optimal number of suppliers? (e.g., 70-30 approach)
    a.  When is this decision made?
    b.  How does this vary for each segment?

#### *Evaluation and Selection*

4.  What criteria do you use to assess potential suppliers at each stage?
    a.  Do these criteria vary by segment? If yes, how?
    b.  How are these criteria linked to your organizational and sourcing strategy?
5.  How are these criteria selected (and weighted)? Who develops the criteria (and weights)?
6.  Who evaluates the potential suppliers? At what stage in the evaluation? (e.g., supply management personnel, cross-functional teams, commodity councils)
7.  Does your supply market research process involve site visits?
    a.  When is a site visit necessary?
    b.  During which stage is the site visit conducted?
    c.  What factors are evaluated during site visits?
    d.  Which personnel comprise the site visit team? How are they selected?
8.  Does your enterprise evaluate existing suppliers differently than new suppliers?
    a.  If yes, describe any differences.

#### *Development and Management*

9.  What is the turnover in your supply base?
10. What occasions turnover? (e.g., regular review, adverse event)
    a.  Who initiates the change? (e.g., you, the supplier)
11. Do you engage in continuous supply market research (i.e., market surveillance) to ensure that your supply base remains optimal?

    a.  If yes, what market surveillance is conducted to ensure that the supply base remains optimal?

12. Do you engage in supplier development activities?
    a.  What are your main supplier development activities?
    b.  Who initiates these activities?
    c.  In what areas do suppliers need the most help?
13. What steps, if any, do you take to assist problematic suppliers before replacing them?

## E.    Other Best-Practices Firms

1. Which firms do you consider as exemplars in market/industry/supplier research?
2. Which firms do you benchmark for market/industry/supplier research?

## F.    What should we have asked that we did not?

# The Sourcing Strategy

This monograph outlines a composite process for market research that moves from a broad industry analysis to evaluation of individual suppliers and then to post-selection supplier management and development. We assume that the enterprise has in place a sourcing strategy. But the analysis outlined in the previous chapters is also useful for *developing and updating* the sourcing strategy. This appendix expands on the sourcing strategy component of Chapter Two and summarizes the options for each element of the sourcing strategy from Raedels, 2000, and Burt, Dobler, and Starling, 2003. We discuss the sourcing strategy components further in this appendix in order to highlight how each of the decisions in the sourcing strategy relies on market research. The enterprise cannot make the optimal decision regarding the buying policy, number of sources, type of source, and supplier relationship without market research on the industry, suppliers, and product.

The first decision in the sourcing strategy is to determine whether to make or buy the required product. The *make-or-buy decision* is a function of the enterprise's core capabilities and available capacity *relative* to that of suppliers. Most enterprises do not have the capabilities or capacity to produce all their necessary inputs. Even when the enterprise does have both the capability and capacity to produce the good or service, buying may remain the preferred option because suppliers may offer a higher-quality, more technologically advanced, or less costly alternative. An important element in the decision is the strategic importance of the purchase. Enterprises with the appropriate capabilities and capacity may prefer to control production of certain key inputs despite other considerations (e.g., costs). Clearly, these issues are informed by the analyses outlined in this monograph.

If the decision is made to buy the product, the enterprise must develop a sourcing strategy. As noted in Chapter Two, the goal of the sourcing strategy depends on the competitive strategy. A low-cost, best-value, or best-quality sourcing strategy may be appropriate depending on the enterprise's organizational goals. An enterprise with a low-price organizational strategy may choose a low-cost sourcing strategy, while an enterprise with a high-quality niche for its product may choose a best-value sourcing strategy. The sourcing strategy primarily encompasses the elements listed in Table B.1.

Regardless of the sourcing approach, consolidating purchases increases the enterprise's leverage with its suppliers. In addition, limiting the number of contracts with each supplier reduces transaction costs (e.g., administrative costs) for both the enterprise and the supplier.

**Table B.1**
**Sourcing Strategy Components**

| Buying Policy | Number of Sources | Type of Source | Supplier Relationship |
|---|---|---|---|
| Subsistence | Sole | Proprietary information | Transactional |
| Forward | Single | Directed sourcing | Ongoing |
| Volume purchase agreement | Multiple | Manufacturer versus distributor | |
| | | Large versus small | |
| Consignment | | Minority | |
| Life-of-product supply | | Local, national, or international suppliers | |
| End-of-life buy | | Cooperative/leveraged, joint venture, or integrated supply | |

SOURCE: Adapted with permission from Alan R. Raedels, *The Supply Management Process: Managing Key Supply Processes,* Tempe, Ariz.: Institute for Supply Management, Inc.,™ 2000, p. 79 (Exhibit 4.1).

Enterprises often consolidate buys from a supplier not only within but also across commodities. Suppliers benefit at the expense of the enterprise from a "divide-and-conquer" approach, which allows them to deal separately with each part of the enterprise. By creating a single point of interaction between the enterprise and the supplier, the enterprise can leverage its buy. To leverage spend fully, the enterprise must understand what it spends, with whom, and on what goods and services via a spend analysis. Of course, new purchases will need to be made on an ongoing basis. However, these can be treated as additions to the existing contract between the enterprise and the supplier.[1]

Using the results of its market research, the enterprise must understand the product offerings, capabilities, and capacities of individual suppliers and how the market for critical items may change over time. Market research will also indicate industry norms for these choices. For example, industry norms may indicate that volume-price agreements are common.

## Buying Policy[2]

The buying policy describes how the purchase is made. The options range from tactical (or reactive) subsistence buys to proactive strategic arrangements. The choice has implications for the enterprise's production schedules and inventory costs. Crucial information collected in the market research and spend analyses includes the availability of supply in the short and long term, the criticality of the item to production, prices and TCO, demand, supplier characteristics, and inventory costs. The buying policy intrinsically revolves around the timing of

---

[1]  Contract consolidation must account for differences in the type of purchase. A contract for a purchase of a good in production may be quite different from a contract in the design stage. For example, one may be a fixed-price contract and the other a cost-plus contract.

[2]  Raedels, 2000, lists speculative buying as another option for the buying policy. This option involves purchases that exceed forecasted requirements in order to enable the enterprise to use the excess supply at a later date or sell it for a profit. This is not common practice and seems less relevant for the Air Force.

purchases. The timing should ensure that production schedules are not compromised, but also that the enterprise does not incur unnecessary costs. There is a trade-off here. Large quantities of inputs on hand preserve production schedules and reduce costs through volume discounts. But an oversupply on hand incurs inventory costs, which include the cost of accelerated expenditures and storage costs.

### Subsistence Buying

Subsistence buying is a reactive or tactical approach: Purchase only the quantity that is needed at a point in time. Subsistence buying may be appropriate when strategic efforts are not possible or necessary (e.g., unanticipated one-time needs). Subsistence buys should not be confused with lean buys. Lean processes, including JIT systems, have been developed to minimize production delays and inventory costs simultaneously. However, JIT systems require a deeper relationship between the enterprise and its supplier to closely coordinate production, delivery, and quality—traditional arm's length contracts are not capable of supporting JIT. Although both subsistence and JIT approaches limit purchases to current needs, subsistence buying is reactive and tactical (and likely a short-term relationship); thus, it differs substantially from the more proactive, strategic, and longer-term JIT approach to supplier relationships. A JIT approach is also more likely to be used for repeated purchases, while subsistence buys are concentrated on one-time buys.

### Forward Buying

Forward buying includes future purchases in order to secure lower prices and ensure supply availability. This approach is more strategic than subsistence buying but presents a trade-off with inventory costs. Quantities not used in immediate production must be stored at a cost, and there is also a cost associated with the acceleration of expenditures. The anticipated "savings" should exceed 3 percent for each month of extra inventory.

### Volume Purchase Agreements

Volume purchase agreements are an alternative to forward buying that reduce inventory costs. These agreements stipulate the total volume to be purchased over a time period or a step function of price versus quantities. Because demand forecasts are often uncertain, enterprises often specify a relationship between price and quantity or provide a best estimate rather than commit to exact purchase quantities. Market research should highlight opportunities for price-quantity trade-offs (e.g., existence of economies of scale and batch production).

### Consignment (and Vendor-Managed Inventory)

Consignment and vendor-managed inventory allow the enterprise to stock goods at its own location before making the purchase. The supplier does not charge the enterprise for the item until it is withdrawn from inventory. This approach assures the enterprise of availability on-site without the inventory cost associated with forward buying.

### Life-of-Product Supply

Life-of-product supply enables the enterprise to ensure supply and potentially negotiate on low-demand items by making the supplier its single source for the life of the product.

### End-of-Life Buy

End-of-life buy is an opportunity for the enterprise to make a last purchase of an item before it is discontinued. The decision depends on the opportunity to purchase from resellers, ability to manufacture in-house, criticality of the good, availability of substitutes, internal demand, inventory costs, and related factors (e.g., goals regarding customer support).

## Number of Suppliers

Enterprises have recently engaged in supply base rationalization. Supply base rationalization is based in part on the potential cost savings from reducing transaction costs, leveraging spend with key suppliers, and developing deeper relationships with key suppliers. Although rationalization is often associated with simply reducing the number of suppliers, it is in fact more about having the *appropriate* number of suppliers. Rationalization efforts have led commercial enterprises to select $n$ suppliers for a good or service, where $n$ is the number of suppliers necessary to provide the required quantities. The need to mitigate supply risk has led other commercial enterprises to engage $n + 1$ suppliers so that some excess capacity is included in the supply base. To assess whether sole, single, or multiple sourcing is appropriate, market research must compare the *relative* size of the purchase to supplier capacity with an understanding that it should be large enough to gain supplier responsiveness (to the buyer), but small enough to prevent supplier dependence.

The number of suppliers in the market and the industry structure (e.g., concentration) affect the enterprise's ability to leverage its buy. In an industry with many suppliers, the enterprise may open a purchase to competition to obtain the best value or lowest price. However, supplier power in highly concentrated industries can undermine buyer efforts. Market research efforts described in previous chapters will identify the number and identity of potential suppliers as well as their production capabilities and capacities. These data can be used to calculate the concentration of production and to indicate relative supplier and purchaser bargaining power. If there is only a single supplier, the enterprise does not have a choice of suppliers in the short term. Negotiation is still possible, but it depends on the buyer's leverage and, in some cases, may focus on factors other than price. The enterprise should, however, remain abreast of changes in market conditions that would indicate entry by new suppliers or an opportunity to develop new suppliers. Market research also provides the necessary information regarding potential entry and long-run conditions. For example, market research may reveal the imminent expiration of the sole supplier's patent or the emergence of a new technology, which would indicate the potential for a change in the number of suppliers. In the long run, the enterprise may also work to develop alternate sources of supply, perhaps among suppliers with similar technologies or manufacturing processes (e.g., supplier development). Lufthansa and American Airlines partnered in Heico Corporation for parts manufacturer approval parts that could compete with original equipment manufacturer (OEM) parts (Davies, 2004).

### Sole Sourcing

Sole sourcing occurs when the market consists of only one supplier. A market may have only a single supplier when barriers to entry or other factors such as patents limit entry. Lack of competition increases the importance of market research—particularly research regarding should-cost and TCO analyses. To avoid sole sourcing, the enterprise may standardize its requirements as much as is feasible.[3]

### Single Sourcing

Single sourcing is the enterprise's decision to use only one supplier even though multiple suppliers exist. Single sourcing can be used to control costs and quality, engage a supplier in research and development, protect proprietary information, limit capitalization costs (e.g., tooling), and leverage volume. Market research is essential to mitigating the risks of supply interruptions, controlling costs, and maintaining performance. There is minimal risk to single sourcing if the good or service is easily obtained from other suppliers (e.g., when the market is perfectly competitive).

### Multiple Sourcing

Multiple sourcing distributes the purchase across several suppliers to reduce the risk of supplier dependence, avoid supply interruptions, and ensure a competitive price. However, with multiple sourcing, there is potential for variation in quality and delivery. Market research is necessary to determine whether multiple sourcing is appropriate. These conditions revolve around capacity, costs, and geographic needs. If market research reveals the potential for supplier dependence, limited industry capacity, lack of price-volume discounts, and location-specific needs, multiple sourcing may be appropriate. Market research will make clear which, if any, of these benefits and risks will materialize. For example, multiple sources may not result in a competitive price if the market is oligopolistic (e.g., the market consists of a limited number of suppliers with market power) and output is constrained to increase prices. On the other hand, in a perfectly competitive market for a standardized commodity, multiple sourcing may not reduce leverage.

## Type of Source

The commodity team must consider proprietary information, socioeconomic goals, supplier size, and geographic concerns when deciding on the type of source. Market research on the

---

[3] The enterprise may also engage in supplier development activities to increase the number of suppliers. Supplier development may require substantial resources and so depends on the resulting benefits.

industry and suppliers—including pricing, quality, product differentiation, and supplier size—is fundamental to this decision.

### Proprietary Information

Proprietary information is the enterprise's private information, such as technical specifications, patented designs, and strategic plans. Safeguarding proprietary information may limit the optimal number of suppliers. For example, a buyer with geographically distributed plants may choose a single national supplier instead of several local suppliers.

### Manufacturer Versus Distributor

The choice to use a manufacturer or a distributor as a supplier depends on the relative importance to the buyer of price versus other terms of the purchase. Manufacturers can offer lower prices for volume purchases, but distributors can allow smaller purchases and offer support services (e.g., customization and integration).

### Supplier Size

Large suppliers have the advantage of more capacity to accommodate increases in demand. However, it is important to distinguish between size and available capacity. A large supplier may have less *available capacity* than smaller suppliers. Also, supplier size can be detrimental if it slows response time. The enterprise should consider the size of its purchase relative to the supplier's overall sales. A sufficiently large buy allows the enterprise some leverage over the supplier to secure prices, quality, and delivery. If the enterprise's purchase is only a small share of a large supplier's production, there is limited incentive for the supplier to accommodate or be responsive to the enterprise.

Small suppliers may value the buyer more highly, offer specialized expertise or quicker response, be appropriate for smaller purchases, and satisfy socioeconomic goals. However, the enterprise should avoid creating supplier dependence by limiting the percentage of the supplier's capacity allocated to the enterprise. This is critical to the enterprise for maintaining its option to react to changing market conditions and move its purchase freely among suppliers. A common rule of thumb is for the buyer not to exceed 25 percent of the supplier's total capacity.[4]

### Small, Minority-, and Women-Owned Suppliers (Diversity Suppliers)

The Air Force, like enterprises with similar socioeconomic concerns, supports diversity suppliers. Commercial enterprises may have mandatory or voluntary socioeconomic goals regarding diversity suppliers. Goals to include or mentor small, disadvantaged, minority-, or women-owned suppliers must be guided by the strategic goals of the enterprise (e.g., key performance indicators) and must be informed by the market research process.[5] Commercial efforts to sup-

---

[4]  Burt, Dobler, and Starling, 2003, recommend a limit of 15 to 25 percent.

[5]  In some cases, enterprises passed these requirements on to their first-tier suppliers. Such an approach is useful when market research indicates that small, minority, and disadvantaged business goals cannot be met because of the type of product purchased (e.g., the purchase of a major subassembly).

port diversity include such developmental efforts as education and training. Technical and financial assistance programs are offered by some larger enterprises.

### Local, National, and International Suppliers

Local suppliers can be more responsive and have lower transportation costs. However, national and international suppliers have the ability to provide goods and services to multiple locations and greater resources to handle unexpected demand. National and international provision eliminates the need to select and manage suppliers at each site, thereby reducing total costs. International suppliers can raise legal, cultural, communication, monetary, and logistics concerns. The Air Force must also consider security concerns and federal regulations.

### Cooperative/Leveraged Buying, Joint Ventures, and Integrated Supply

Cooperative/leveraged buying, joint ventures, and integrated supply are types of joint efforts by two or more enterprises to increase purchasing effectiveness (e.g., via increased purchasing leverage), achieve economies of scale, and reduce risks.

## Supplier Relationships

Traditionally, most supplier relationships have been arm's-length contracts. But more recently, these relationships have become increasingly long term and integrated (with the enterprise). The appropriate choice for the supplier relationship depends on the purchase, industry norms, and the goals and characteristics of the enterprise. The length of the contract is a related decision that is informed by the type of supplier relationship and transaction type as well as industry norms. For example, a strategic relationship should be of sufficient length to promote cooperation and should be based on industry norms or other relevant factors (e.g., on the life of the product). Market research on industry norms will reveal the typical supplier relationship within the industry and help inform the enterprise's decision. Table B.2 provides some additional insights on the proper supplier relationship given the operational characteristics of the purchase.

### Transactional Relationships

Transactional relationships are used for infrequent purchases or purchases in which there is little expectation of ongoing support. For example, a one-time commodity purchase of standardized nails is a transactional purchase. However, a one-time purchase of aircraft engines is not transactional because of the after-market support required.

### Ongoing Relationships

Ongoing relationships are repeated or long-run arrangements that fall into four types based on the level of complexity and mutual dependence. In order of increasing complexity and mutual dependence, the four types are contractual relationships, operational relationships, business relationships, and strategic relationships (or alliances).

**Table B.2**
**Matrix Linking Supplier Relationship to the Operational Characteristics of the Purchase**

| Operational Characteristic | Type of Supplier Relationship | | | |
| --- | --- | --- | --- | --- |
| | Vendor | Preferred Supplier | Exclusive Supplier | Partner |
| Strategic importance | Low | High | Low | High |
| Buyer's bargaining power | High | High | Low | Low |
| Number of suppliers | Many | Few | One or very few | One or very few |
| Contract type | Purchase orders | Contract | Contract | Agreements |
| Contract length | Short | Medium product life | Medium product life | Long |
| Product/service | Standard | Specialized | Specialized | Cutting edge |
| Information exchange | Sporadic | Frequent (supplier provided regarding cost, process, and quality to the buyer) | Frequent (buyer provided regarding design, sales, cost, and inventory to the supplier) | Continuous, mutual exchange |
| Pricing scheme | Unit price | Unit price plus supplier incentives | Unit price plus buyer sales incentives | Risk and profit sharing |
| Delivery schedule | Infrequent | Frequent | Frequent | Very frequent |
| Senior management involvement | Not necessary | Necessary | Necessary | Critical |
| Supplier development programs | No | No | Yes | Yes |

SOURCE: Adapted from Christopher Tang, "Supplier Relationship Map," *International Journal of Logistics: Research and Applications*, Vol. 2, No. 1, April 1999, Table 3. Used by permission from Taylor & Francis Ltd., http://www.tandf.co.uk/journals/.

Deeper supplier relationships are increasingly common. The most strategic and deepest relationships are supplier alliances. These alliances can promote lower costs, improvements in quality, and other benefits. To achieve these improvements, the supplier and the enterprise must work together to their mutual benefit—a process that requires trust and cooperation (Burt, Dobler, and Starling, 2003). These relationships are often difficult and resource intensive and so are reserved for strategic purchases (Stundza, 2001). The decision to form an alliance depends on the benefits, the willingness (or buy in), competition in the supply market, supplier capabilities, and stability of the market and demand.[6]

Even commercial enterprises that have moved from arms-length to deeper supplier relationships did not do so for all of their suppliers. Rather, the supplier relationship was tailored to the purchase. Table B.2 provides a matrix for assigning the proper supplier relationship given the operational characteristics of the purchase. Deeper supplier relationships are characterized by the strategic importance of the good or service, limited buyer power, limited number of suppliers, differentiated products, frequent purchases, information sharing, supplier development activities, senior management involvement, and specialized contract terms (i.e., length, type, and price terms).

---

[6]  See Burt, Dobler, and Starling, 2003, who summarize Kauffman's work in this area.

# Internet Sources of Information

This appendix provides a list of useful Web sites for market research drawn from Raedels, 2000; Gabbard, 2004; and Leenders et al., 2001. The Internet has become an important source of information. Suppliers, industry and trade associations, domestic sourcing information, international sourcing information, government Web sites, purchasing organizations and periodicals, and materials exchange Web sites now provide information online. This list is organized by the type of source (e.g., industry and trade associations). As discussed in Chapter Three and throughout the document, the utility of a source depends on the information being sought. For example, information on general economic conditions are generally most easily available from government Web sites such as the Bureau of Labor Statistics or the Department of Commerce, while information on industries can be gathered from industry and trade organizations and other third-party observers. Table C.1 provides a sample list of useful online sources for various goods and services. As the commodity team works with its own goods and services, it will develop its own list.

**Table C.1**
**Online Sources of Information**

| Organization | Web Address | Description |
|---|---|---|
| **Industry and Organizations** | | |
| Aluminum Association | www.aluminum.org | Industry news, statistics, and other resources |
| American Chemical Society | www.chemcenter.org | Membership organization that provides a broad range of opportunities for peer interaction and career development |
| American Iron and Steel Institute | www.steel.org | Iron and steel industry developments (news), statistics, and events |
| American National Standards Institute | www.ansi.org | News and publications, education and training, and events |
| American Society of Transportation & Logistics | www.astl.org | Transportation and logistics-related training |
| Electronic Design Automation Consortium | www.edac.org | International association of companies engaged in the development, manufacture, and sale of design tools to the electronic engineering community. Site provides a forum for discussion of industry-wide problems and concerns |

**Table C.1—Continued**

| Organization | Web Address | Description |
| --- | --- | --- |
| Electronic Industries Alliance | www.eia.org | Information on the association and its activities, and links to other related groups, divisions, and associations |
| Industrial Supply Association | www.ida-assoc.org | Information regarding the association's activities, members, and educational programs in industrial distribution |
| Industrial Fasteners Institute | www.industrial-fasteners.org | Information about the institute, technical information, trade show information, and a list of available publications |
| MASSnet Packaging Mall | www.trprint.com/ packaging/links.nsf/0/ 4686DFA9F8F19216C125 6A840039E57D?Open Document | Links to various suppliers and manufacturers of packaging equipment and supplies |
| Material Handling Industry of America | www.mhi.org | Information on trade shows and conferences, upcoming events, literature, and Material Handling Industry publications |
| Metal Suppliers Online | www.suppliersonline. com | A database of metals suppliers |
| Metal Treating Institute | www.metaltreat.com | A metal treating buyers' guide, industry information, and lists of available educational materials |
| Oil and Gas Online | www.oilandgasonline. com | Sourcing directory for oil and gas |
| PartNET | www.part.net | Component information system that allows searching for electromechanical, electronic, and mechanical parts from a number of suppliers simultaneously |
| Precision Metalforming Association | www.pma.org | Buyers' guides and organization information including publications and seminar information |
| SEMATECH | www.sematech.org | List of acronyms and abbreviations, SEMATECH dictionary, information about SEMATECH programs and divisions, job opportunities, and technology transfer information |
| SEMI | www.semi.org | Electronics industry information such as news, business outlook market statistics, newsletters, standards, and trade show information |
| SMTnet | www.smtnet.com | Reference center for surface mount technology and electronics manufacturing. Features a technical library and lists electronics manufacturing supplies, contract manufacturers, component manufacturers, service providers, distributors, and OEMs |
| Steel Manufacturers Association | www.steelnet.org | Information on sources of steel products and steel-making equipment and links to related sites |
| Telecommunications Industry Association | www.tiaonline.org | Information about the Telecommunications Industry Association, trade shows, standards, publications, and links to other sites |

**Table C.1—Continued**

| Organization | Web Address | Description |
|---|---|---|
| **Domestic Sourcing Information** | | |
| American Productivity & Quality Center | www.apqc.org | Management information including benchmarking, best practices, reengineering, and TQM |
| Better Business Bureau | www.bbb.org | Information about business and consumer alerts, a research library, and business reports |
| Companies-Online | www.companies-online.com | Directory of businesses with Web sites. It provides information on over 60,000 companies at no charge |
| D&B | www.dnb.com | Summary reports on millions of companies worldwide. Includes financials and other relevant information |
| EDGAR (U.S. Securities and Exchange Commission) | www.sec.gov/edgar.shtml | All foreign and domestic companies' registration statements, periodic reports, and other forms electronically filed through EDGAR |
| ElectroBase | www.electrobase.com | A comprehensive listing of distributors, representatives, services, and component manufacturers of interest to the electronics industry |
| Electronic Engineers Master | www.eem.com | A subscription service that provides an electronic parts locator database that lists current inventories of franchised dealers |
| Electronics & Engineering Network | www.eenet.com | Online directory for the electronics industry with over 11,000 links |
| Electronics Purchasing Guide to Distribution | www.theepgd.com | A directory of component distributors searchable by region, manufacturer, and distributor |
| Electronics Supply & Manufacturing | www.my-esm.com | Sourcing directory provided by distributors and manufacturers of components that can be searched by product category; information geared toward OEMs |
| FastParts.com | www.fastparts.com | A computer network broker for electronic parts, components, products, test instruments, and laboratory equipment |
| *Inc.* magazine | www.inc.com | Financial and related information on thousands of privately held organizations: profits, revenues, losses, number of employees, etc. The *Inc.* 500 list |
| LogLink | www.loglink.com | Links relating to logistics, logistic references, trucking, and other logistics topics |
| Minority Business & Professional Directory | www.mbpd.com/ | Magazine-style directory of minority- and women-owned businesses |
| SEMATECH | www.sematech.org | List of acronyms and abbreviations, SEMATECH dictionary, information about SEMATECH programs and divisions, job opportunities, and technology transfer information |
| SEMI | www.semi.org | Electronics industry information such as news, business outlook market statistics, newsletters, standards, and trade show information |

**Table C.1—Continued**

| Organization | Web Address | Description |
|---|---|---|
| SemiWeb | www.semiweb.com | Information on companies, employment opportunities, research, and related Web sites for semiconductor-related resources |
| SMTnet | www.smtnet.com | Reference center for surface mount technology and electronics manufacturing. Features a technical library and lists electronics manufacturing supplies, contract manufacturers, component manufacturers, service providers, distributors, and OEMs |
| Steel Manufacturers Association | www.steelnet.org | Information on sources of steel products and steel-making equipment and links to related sites |
| Telecommunications Industry Association | www.tiaonline.org | Information about the Telecommunications Industry Association, trade shows, standards, publications, and links to other sites |
| ThomasNet | www.thomasnet.com | Online search ability of ThomasNet's database, a comprehensive resource for industrial information, products, services, CAD drawings, and "How to Buy It" tutorials |

**International Sourcing Information**

| Organization | Web Address | Description |
|---|---|---|
| All Business | www.allbusiness.com | A global directory with millions of small business listings and links to over 100,000 Web sites in 150 countries |
| Asian Sources Online | www.asia.manufacturers.globalsources.com | Product, supplier, and country searches as well as information on trade shows, travel services, and trade services |
| AsiaOne | www.asia1.com | Links to a variety of resources about Asia, lists of companies in Singapore, and other information |
| Canadian Business and Economics Guide | www.library.ualberta.ca/subject/business/canadianbusiness/index.cfm | Articles, statistics, and other information about Canadian businesses and economic analysis |
| IMEX Exchange | www.imex.com | International business information, including a worldwide database of goods and services |
| LAMIREL PCB Europe | www.lamirel.cz/en/index.html | Information about service providers, manufacturers, electronic design, associations, news/magazines, and Web services |
| Taiwan External Trade Development Council | www.tptaiwan.org.tw | How to use the council's resources, tips on doing business in Taiwan, and trade show information |
| WAND, Inc. | www.wand.com | International business-to-business directory featuring an advanced product and service category system for matching buyers and sellers in every industry |
| WorldPages | www.worldpages.com | An Internet and Yellow Pages directory company with links to international directories |
| Yellow.com | www.yellow.com | Worldwide listing of companies |

**Table C.1—Continued**

| Organization | Web Address | Description |
|---|---|---|
| **Government Web Sites** | | |
| Government Accountability Office | www.gao.gov | Industry reports and related studies |
| National Institute of Standards and Technology (U.S. Department of Commerce) | www.nist.gov | Information and research on industries |
| STAT-USA/Internet (U.S. Department of Commerce) | www.stat-usa.gov | Economic news, statistical releases, databases, and selected publications |
| U.S. Census Bureau, Manufacturing, Mining, and Construction Statistics | www.census.gov/mcd | The bureau's economic census periodically profiles economic activity from the national to the local level |
| U.S. Department of Commerce | www.commerce.gov | Demographics and industry market data |
| U.S. Department of Labor, Bureau of Labor Statistics | www.bls.gov | A government Web site with data on producer and consumer price indexes as well as employment levels and employment compensation indexes |
| U.S. Environmental Protection Agency | www.epa.gov | Environmental regulations and issues |
| U.S. Internal Revenue Service | www.irs.gov | Industry and enterprise information |
| U.S. International Trade Commission | www.usltc.gov | Trade resources, news reports, and publications |
| World Trade Organization | www.wto.org | Information on international trade, trade policy reviews, press releases, and publications |
| **Purchasing Organizations and Periodicals** | | |
| APICS (American Production and Inventory Control Society) | www.apics.org | Training, seminars, certification programs, and other events |
| CAPS (Center for Advanced Purchasing Studies) Research | www.capsresearch.org | Research and publications to support continuous change and performance improvement in strategic sourcing and supply |
| Council of Supply Chain Management Professionals (formerly, Council of Logistics Management) | www.cscmp.org | Research and conferences on logistics and supply chain management |
| GS1 UK | www.gs1uk.org.uk | UK business association specializing in cross-sector supply chain standards, from bar coding to electronic business communications |
| *Inside Supply Management* | www.ism.ws | *Inside Supply Management* magazine published by the Institute for Supply Management (ISM) |
| Institute for Supply Management (ISM) | www.ism.ws | Conferences, publications, and education for purchasing and supply chain professionals |
| International Warehouse Logistics Association (Association for Logistics Outsourcing) | www.iwla.com | Membership of third-party warehousing, transportation, and logistics service providers |

**Table C.1—Continued**

| Organization | Web Address | Description |
|---|---|---|
| IOMA Inc. | www.ioma.com | Business articles and news |
| MagPortal | www.magportal.com | Portal to articles with searchable text |
| National Contract Management Association | www.ncmahq.org | Education, certification, conferences, and publications on contract management |
| Outsourcing Institute | www.outsourcing.com | Outsourcing Web site targeting buyers and providers |
| Purchasing magazine | www.purchasing.com | Web site for Purchasing magazine with news and articles on supply chains, purchasing, and logistics |
| Society of Competitive Intelligence Professionals | www.scip.org | Assistance, articles, and advice |
| Ziff Davis Media Publications | www.zdnet.com | Online magazines and e-commerce information |

SOURCES: Adapted from Raedels, 2000, Appendix 4-A, pp. 105ff; Gabbard, 2004; Leenders et al., 2001; Burt, Dobler, and Starling, 2003; and Nordstrom and Pinkerton, 1999.

# Sources for Researching Financial Status

Supplier financial analyses are critical to evaluating suppliers. In this appendix, we list online sources for financial information (see Table D.1) and provide additional detail on the calculation and interpretation of financial measures (Table D.2). The information is drawn from

**Table D.1**
**Sources of Financial Data**

| Organization | Web Address | Description |
|---|---|---|
| D&B | www.dnb.com | Short reports on millions of companies worldwide. Credit reports available by subscription |
| *Forbes* | www.forbes.com | Basic financial information on companies |
| *Fortune* | www.fortune.com | Financial information for Fortune 500 companies |
| Hoover's Online | www.hoovers.com | Detailed income statement and balance sheet information for 2,500 organizations |
| *Inc.* magazine | www.inc.com/ | Financial and related information on thousands of privately held organizations: profits, revenues, losses, number of employees, etc. The Inc. 500 list |
| Moody's Industrials | www.moodys.com | Credit ratings, research and risk analysis, credit opinions, deal research, and commentary |
| Reuters.com | www.investor.reuters.com/ | Financial information on publicly traded companies |
| Standard & Poor's | www.compustat.com | In-depth strategic financial information for institutional investors |
| Thomson Corporation | www.thomson.com/financial/financial.jsp | Provider of independent credit ratings, indexes, investment research, and valuations |
| U.S. Department of Commerce | www.commerce.gov | Demographics and industry market data of commerce collected by the U.S. government |
| U.S. Securities and Exchange Commission | www.sec.gov (www.sec.gov/edgar.shtml) | The EDGAR database |
| Yahoo! Finance | http://finance.yahoo.com | Financial and stocks news |

SOURCES: Raedels, 2000 p. 151; Monczka, Trent, and Handfield, 2001; Hollingsworth, 1998; Burt, Dobler, and Starling, 2003; and Nordstrom and Pinkerton, 1999.

Raedels, 2000; Monczka, Trent, and Handfield, 2001; Hollingsworth, 1998; Burt, Dobler, and Starling, 2003; and Nordstrom and Pinkerton, 1999. Some of the Web sites offer information free of charge, while others provide information for a fee or subscription.

**Table D.2**
**Interpreting Key Financial Ratios**

| Liquidity Ratios | Interpretation |
|---|---|
| Current ratio = current assets/current liabilities | Should be over 1.0, but look at industry average; high—may mean poor asset management |
| Quick ratio = (cash + receivables)/current liabilities | At least 0.8 if supplier sells on credit; low—may mean cash flow problems; high—may mean poor asset management |
| *Note: Calculation includes marketable securities* | |

| Activity Ratios | |
|---|---|
| Inventory turnover = cost of goods sold/ inventory | Compare industry average; low—problems with slow inventory, which may hurt cash flow |
| Fixed asset turnover = sales/fixed assets | Compare industry average; too low may mean supplier is not using fixed assets efficiently or effectively |
| Total asset turnover = sales/total assets | Compare industry average; too low may mean supplier is not using total assets efficiently or effectively |
| Days sales outstanding = (receivables*365) sales | Compare industry average, or a value of 45–50 if company sells on net 30; too high hurts cash flow; too low may mean credit policies to customers are too restrictive |

| Profitability Ratios | |
|---|---|
| Net profit margin= profit after taxes/sales | Compare industry average |
| Return on assets = profit after taxes/total assets | Compare industry average; represents the return the company earns on everything it owns |
| Return on equity = profit after taxes/equity | The higher the better; the return on the shareholders' investment in the business |
| Debt ratios | |
| Debt to equity = total liabilities/equity | Compare industry average; over 3 means highly leveraged |
| Current debt to equity = current liabilities/equity | Over 1 is risky unless the industry average is over 1; when ratio is high, supplier may be unable to pay lenders |
| Interest coverage = (pretax income + interest expense)/interest expense | Should be over 3; higher is better; low may mean supplier is having difficulty paying creditors |

SOURCE: Adapted from *Purchasing and Supply Chain Management,* 2nd ed., by Monczka, Trent, and Handfield, p. 240. © 2002. Reprinted with permission of South-Western, a division of Thomson Learning: www.thomsonrights. com. Fax 800-730-2215.

# Supplier Evaluation Tools

Chapter Five highlighted a number of areas in which suppliers may be evaluated. This appendix provides sample templates for evaluation that touch upon a number of these areas. These templates are drawn from a number of sources including Raedels, 2000; Wehr, 1992; Burt, Dobler, and Starling, 2003; and Monczka, Trent, and Handfield, 2001.

## Evaluating Supplier Quality, Organization, and Management

### Supplier Quality

The following provides evaluation of supplier quality (adapted from Wehr, 1992):

### *Internal Operations*

- Does management provide quality leadership?
- What is the extent of quality commitment?
- Are there quality control points in all processes?
- Are employees at all levels able to relate the tasks they perform to meeting customer needs?

### *Continuing Process Improvements*

- Are there specific results attributable to the quality improvement process?
- Are there documented improvements in methods and processes?
- Are future improvements documented and methods established to ensure improvements will be implemented?

### *Performance Measurement and Tracking*

- Can data be collected to support measures such as on-time delivery, shipping discrepancies, invoice accuracy, and line item fill rates?
- Are performance indicators established for all partnering agreements?

### Problem Solving Capabilities

- Is there a preventive action orientation rather than a reactive response to problems?
- Is problem solving performed in a timely and conclusive manner?
- Are employees at all levels involved in identifying and solving problems?
- Employee participation and involvement
- Is there active participation and involvement by all employees in the quality process?
- Are employees empowered to take action?

### Procedure Development

- Are written procedures established for all processes?
- Are procedures consistently followed?

### Training

- Is a continuous quality training program in place and operational?

### Other Issues

- *Acceptance/Rejection History*—review records, check device calibrations.
- *Testing Capabilities*—sampling techniques; examination of final products; written quality control procedures; compatible (to purchaser) methods, procedures, and instruments; current calibration dates; shop floor quality checks; and process documentation, identified quality control points, and ability to collect data to support quality measures.
- *Process Control*—quality detection and correction systems.
- *Organization and Management of Quality Systems*—proactive versus reactive quality systems; written inspection procedures; solid training; certification (ISO-9000 or Malcolm Baldridge National Quality Award).

## Supplier Organization and Management

The following evaluation areas for supplier organization and management are recommended (adapted from Raedels, 2000, pp. 164ff):

- Training of sales people
- Technical support provided to the sales force and the customer
- Employee attitudes and overall interest in your business
- History and stability of supplier
- Background of key personnel
- Ownership involvement of top management. Specifically:
  - Education, background, and turnover of management staff
  - Management policies and future plans
  - Employee skills, training, experience, competence, turnover

- Education, prior work experience, and length of employment of technical personnel
- A well-documented training program and frequency and level of training
- Workforce diversity and equal employment opportunity violations
- A review of subcontractors and overlap of contractors with purchaser suppliers.

• Supplier labor status
  - Union, nonunion, or mixed labor force
  - Labor-management relations
  - Expiration date of current labor contract.
  - Information about recent contract negotiations (e.g., strikes).

• Other factors
  - Third-party evaluations—can be useful for avoiding costly analyses
  - Major manufacturers—use a supplier that has already been certified by major organizations (e.g., Ford, Motorola, etc.)
  - Federal, state, or local government-qualified bidder list—use government's prequalified list
  - ISO-9000—useful for quality control system issues, but does not address suitability of that supplier for a particular purchaser
  - Logistical concerns—experience with special logistical concerns (e.g., permits and transportation)
  - Environmental performance—previous violations or fines, government closure, and employee exposure and safety record.

## Supplier Plant Survey

Table E.1 and the following text provide an example of a plant survey based on Appendix A of Burt, Dobler, and Starling, 2003, pp. 349ff. (See Burt, Dobler, and Starling for a more complete description of the areas.) The survey is for critical products and, as such, is intensive. The survey requires the team to provide a yes or no response or a rating from 1 to 10 for each of the areas of evaluation. As with all performance rating programs, ratings must also be defined. This example defines each of the ratings from 1 to 10.

**Table E.1**
**Ratings for the Illustrative Plant Survey**

| Rating | Description |
|--------|-------------|
| 10 | The provision or conditions are extensive and function is excellent |
| 9 | The provision or conditions are moderately extensive and function is excellent |
| 8 | The provision or conditions are extensive and are functioning well |
| 6/7 | The provision or conditions are moderately extensive and functioning well |
| 4/5 | The provisions or conditions are limited in extent but are functioning well |
| 2/3 | The provisions or conditions are moderately extensive but are functioning poorly |
| 1 | The provisions or conditions are limited in extent and are functioning poorly |
| 0 | The provisions or conditions are missing but needed |

SOURCE: Burt, Dobler, and Starling, 2003, pp. 355ff. *World Class Supply Management: The Key to Supply Chain Management, 7th ed.,* © The McGraw-Hill Companies, Inc., 2003. Used by permission.

## Design Information

1.  ( )  How well do procedures cover the release, change, and recall of design and manufacturing information, including correlation of customer specifications, and how well are procedures followed?
2.  ( )  How well do records reflect the incorporation of changes?
3.  ( )  How well does quality control verify that changes are incorporated at the effective points?
4.  ( )  Is the design of experiments employed to ensure robust designs prior to the release of designs to manufacturing and supply management?
5.  ( )  How well is the control of design and manufacturing information applied to the procurement activity?
6.  (Y/N) Is there a formal deviation procedure, and how well is it followed?
7.  (Y/N) Does your company have a written system for incorporating customer changes into shop drawings?
8.  (Y/N) Does your company have a reliability department?
9.  (Y/N) Are reliability data used in developing new designs?
10. (Y/N) Is quality history fed back to engineering for improvements in current or future designs? Does quality management review new designs?
11. (Y/N) Does your company have a sample or prototype department?
12. (Y/N) Does Q.A. review sample prototypes?
13. (Y/N) Is this information used in developing shop inspection instructions?
14. (Y/N) Are customer specifications interpreted into shop specifications?
15. (Y/N) Do drawings and specifications accompany purchase orders to suppliers?
16. (Y/N) Are these reviewed by quality management?
17. (Y/N) Are characteristics classified on the engineering documents as to importance?

18.   (Y/N) Does Q.A. review new drawings with the intent of designing and gauging fixtures?

## Procurement-Control of Purchased Material

19.   ( )   How well are potential suppliers evaluated and monitored?
20.   ( )   How well are quality requirements specified?
21.   ( )   How well are inspection procedures specified, and how well are they followed?
22.   ( )   How adequate are inspection facilities and equipment?
23.   ( )   Have you certified (approved) key suppliers' design manufacturing and quality processes so that their shipments to you do not require inspection and testing?
24.   ( )   How adequate are "certifications" which are used in lieu of inspection?
25.   ( )   How well are certifications evaluated by independent checking?
26.   ( )   How well are inspection results used for corrective action?
27.   (Y/N) Do you have an incoming inspection department (If yes, list personnel)
Inspectors _____ Supervisors _____
Quality Engineers _____
28.   (Y/N) Are purchase orders made available to incoming inspection?
29.   (Y/N) Is there a system for keeping shop drawings up to date?
30.   (Y/N) Are written inspection instructions available?
31.   (Y/N) Is sample inspection used?
32.   (Y/N) Is gauging equipment calibrated periodically?
33.   (Y/N) Is gauging equipment correlated with suppliers' equipment?
34.   (Y/N) Are suppliers' test records used for acceptance?
35.   (Y/N) Are commercial test records used for acceptance?
36.   (Y/N) Is material identified to physical and chemical test reports?
37.   (Y/N) Are records kept to show acceptance and rejection of incoming material?
38.   (Y/N) Does your company have a supplier rating system?
39.   (Y/N) Is it made available to the supply management department?
40.   (Y/N) Is the supplier notified of nonconforming material?
41.   (Y/N) Does your company have an approved supplier list?
42.   (Y/N) Does your company survey supplier facilities?
43.   (Y/N) Does the incoming inspection department have adequate storage space to hold material until it is inspected?
44.   (Y/N) Is nonconforming material identified as such?
45.   (Y/N) Is nonconforming material held in a specific area until disposition can be made? Who is responsible for making disposition of nonconforming material?

_____

## Material Control

46.   ( )   How adequate are procedures for storage, release, and movement of material, and how well are they followed?
47.   ( )   How well are incoming materials quarantined while under test?
48.   ( )   How well are materials in stores identified and controlled?

49. ( ) How well are in-process materials identified and controlled?
50. ( ) How well are materials in inspection identified and controlled?
51. ( ) How adequate are storage areas and facilities?
52. ( ) How well is access to material controlled?
53. ( ) How well do procedures cover the prevention of corrosion, deterioration, or damage of material and finished goods?
54. ( ) How well are they followed?
55. ( ) How well are nonconforming items identified, isolated, and controlled?

## Manufacturing Control

56. ( ) How well are process capabilities established and maintained?
57. ( ) How well is in-process inspection specified?
58. ( ) How effectively is it performed?
59. ( ) How adequate are inspection facilities and equipment?
60. ( ) How well are the results of in-process inspection used in the promotion of effective corrective action?
61. ( ) How adequate are equipment and facilities maintained?
62. ( ) How adequate are housekeeping procedures, and how well are they followed?
63. ( ) Does your company have a process inspection function? (If yes, list on a separate sheet inspectors, supervisory and quality engineering personnel.) To whom does process inspection report? _____
64. (Y/N) Are inspection stations located in the production area?
65. (Y/N) Are shop drawings and specifications available to inspection?
66. (Y/N) Is there a system for reviewing and updating inspection instructions?
67. (Y/N) Are written inspection instructions available?
68. (Y/N) Is there a system for reviewing and updating inspection instructions?
69. (Y/N) Is sample inspection used?
70. (Y/N) Do production workers inspect their own work?
71. (Y/N) Are inspection records kept on file?
72. (Y/N) Is inspection equipment calibrated periodically?
73. (Y/N) Is all material identified (route tags, etc.)?
74. (Y/N) Is defective material identified as such?
75. (Y/N) Is defective material segregated from good material until disposition is made?
76. (Y/N) Are first production parts inspected before a job can be run?
77. (Y/N) Is corrective action taken to prevent the recurrence of defective material?
78. (Y/N) Who is responsible for making disposition of nonconforming material?
79. (Y/N) Does your company use x-bar and R charts?
80. (Y/N) Does your company use process capability studies?
81. (Y/N) Are standards calibrated by an outside source that certifies traceability to NBS?
82. (Y/N) Are standards calibrated directly by NBS?
83. (Y/N) Are packaged goods checked for proper packaging?

**Quality Management**

84. (Y/N) Does the potential supplier embrace total quality management?
85. (Y/N) How adequate is the quality philosophy, and how well is it explained in operating policies and procedures?
86. (Y/N) How adequate is the technical competence in the quality discipline of those responsible for assuring quality?
87. (Y/N) How well does the organizational structure define quality responsibility and authority?
88. (Y/N) How well does the organizational structure provide access to top management?
89. (Y/N) How adequate is the documentation and dissemination of quality control procedures?
90. (Y/N) How adequate is the training program, including employee records?

Does the quality department have:

91. (Y/N) A written quality policy and procedures manual?
92. (Y/N) Written inspection instructions?
93. (Y/N) A quality engineering department?
94. (Y/N) A person or persons who perform(s) vendor surveys?
95. (Y/N) An incoming inspection department?
96. (Y/N) An in-process inspection department?
97. (Y/N) A final inspection department? To whom does the inspection department report? _____
98. (Y/N) A quality audit function?
99. (Y/N) A gauge control program?
100. (Y/N) A gauge control laboratory?
101. (Y/N) Other quality laboratories? (If yes, specify type) _____
102. (Y/N) A quality cost program?
103. (Y/N) A reliability department?
104. (Y/N) Does the quality department use statistical tools (control charts, sampling plans, etc.)? Explain _____
105. (Y/N) Is government sources inspection available to your plant? Resident _____ _____ Itinerant _____ No _____

**Quality Information**

106. ( ) How well are records of inspection maintained?
107. ( ) How adequate is the record and sample retention program?
108. ( ) How well are quality data used as a basis for action?
109. ( ) How well are quality data used in supporting certification of quality furnished to customers? How well is customer and field information used for corrective action?
110. ( ) How well is it reported to management?

**Calibration—Inspection and Testing**

111.   ( )   How well do internal standards conform to national standards or customer standards?
112.   ( )   How well are periodic inspections and calibrations specified?
113.   ( )   How adequate are calibration facilities and equipment?
114.   ( )   If external calibration sources are utilized, how adequate is the program and how well is it executed?
115.   (Y/N) Does your company have a gauge control function?
116.   (Y/N) Does your company have written instructions for operating inspection and test instruments?
117.   (Y/N) Are all inspection instruments calibrated at periodic intervals?
118.   (Y/N) Are records of calibration kept on file?
119.   (Y/N) Is there a system to recall inspection instruments when they are due for calibration?
120.   (Y/N) Are the inspection instruments used by production calibrated?
121.   (Y/N) If so, are these instruments removed from use until they can be repaired or recalibrated?
122.   (Y/N) Are shop maters calibrated at periodic intervals to secondary standards traceable to NBS?

**Inspection of Completed Material**

123.   (Y/N) Does your company have a final inspection function? If yes, list inspection, supervisory, and quality engineers on a separate sheet. To whom does the final inspection department report? _____
124.   (Y/N) Are shop drawings and specifications available to inspection?
125.   (Y/N) Is there a system for keeping the documents up to date?
126.   (Y/N) Are written inspection instructions available?
127.   (Y/N) Is there a system for reviewing and updating inspection instructions?
128.   (Y/N) Is sample inspection used?
129.   (Y/N) Are inspection records kept on file?
130.   (Y/N) Are records of inspection results used for corrective-action purposes?
131.   (Y/N) Is inspection equipment calibrated periodically?
132.   (Y/N) Is all material identified (route tags, etc.)?
133.   (Y/N) Is defective material identified as such?
134.   (Y/N) Is defective material segregated from good material until disposition is made?
135.   (Y/N) Who is responsible for making disposition of nonconforming material? _____
136.   (Y/N) Is reworked material submitted for reinspection?

**Final Acceptance**

137.   (Y/N) How well are specifications used in determining the acceptability of material?
138.   (Y/N) How well are certifications and in-process inspection records used in the final acceptance decisions?

139. (Y/N) How adequate are inspection procedures? How well are they followed?
140. (Y/N) How adequate are inspection facilities and equipment?
141. (Y/N) How well are inspection results used for corrective action?
142. (Y/N) How adequate are packing and order-checking procedures?
143. (Y/N) How well are they followed?

When evaluating a new supplier for a critical purchase, the enterprise needs to develop a scorecard to rate key performance areas. Table E.1 from Monczka, Trent, and Handfield,

**Table E.2**
**Initial Supplier Evaluation**

| Category | Weight | Subweight | Score (5 pt. scale) | Weighted score | |
|---|---|---|---|---|---|
| 1. Quality Systems | 20 | | | | |
|   Process control systems | | 5 | 4 | 4.0 | |
|   Total quality commitment | | 8 | 4 | 6.4 | |
|   Parts per million defect performance | | 7 | 5 | 7.0 | 17.4 |
| 2. Management Capability | 10 | | | | |
|   Management/labor relations | | 5 | 4 | 4.0 | |
|   Management capability | | 5 | 4 | 4.0 | 8.0 |
| 3. Financial Condition | 10 | | | | |
|   Debt structure | | 5 | 3 | 3.0 | |
|   Turnover ratios | | 5 | 4 | 4.0 | 7.0 |
| 4. Cost Structure | 15 | | | | |
|   Costs relative to industry | | 5 | 5 | 5.0 | |
|   Understanding of costs | | 5 | 4 | 4.0 | |
|   Cost control/reduction efforts | | 5 | 5 | 5.0 | 14.0 |
| 5. Delivery Performance | 15 | | | | |
|   Performance to promise | | 5 | 3 | 3.0 | |
|   Lead-time requirements | | 5 | 3 | 3.0 | |
|   Responsiveness | | 5 | 3 | 3.0 | 9.0 |
| 6. Technical/Process Capability | 15 | | | | |
|   Product innovation | | 5 | 4 | 4.0 | |
|   Process innovation | | 5 | 5 | 5.0 | |
|   Research and development | | 5 | 5 | 5.0 | 14.0 |
| 7. Information Systems Capability | 5 | | | | |
|   EDI capability | | 3 | 5 | 3.0 | |
|   CAD/CAM | | 2 | 0 | 0.0 | 3.0 |
| 8. General | 10 | | | | |
|   Support of minority suppliers | | 2 | 3 | 1.2 | |
|   Environmental compliance | | 3 | 5 | 3.0 | |
|   Supplier's supply-base management | | 5 | 4 | 4.0 | 8.2 |
| Total Weighted Score | | | | | 80.6 |

SOURCE: From *Purchasing and Supply Chain Managment*, 2nd ed., by Monczka, Trent, and Handfield, Exhibit 8.7, p. 246, © 2002. Reprinted with permission of South-Western, a division of Thomson Learning: www.thomsonrights. com. Fax 800-730-2215.

NOTES: EDI = electronic data interchange; CAD/CAM = computer-aided design and computer-aided manufacturing.

RAND *MG473-TE.2*

2001, provides an example of an initial supplier evaluation form. The form lists eight factors for evaluation—each factor is formed from several criteria. Weights are assigned to each of the criteria within a factor. Factor weights are generated by aggregating the weights from the individual criterion. Each criterion is scored individually. Scores are aggregated to the factor-level and then to an overall score using the assigned weights.

# Bibliography

Air Force Materiel Command, *AFMC Commercial Acquisition Guide,* Wright-Patterson AFB, Ohio: Air Force Materiel Command, 1998.

Ausink, John A., Laura H. Baldwin, Sarah Hunter, and Chad Shirley, *Implementing Performance-Based Services Acquisition (PBSA): Perspectives from an Air Logistics Center and a Product Center,* Santa Monica, Calif.: RAND Corporation, DB-388-AF, 2002. Online at www.rand. org/pubs/documented_briefings/DB388.

Ausink, John A., Laura H. Baldwin, and Christopher Paul, *Air Force Procurement Workforce Transformation: Lessons from the Commercial Sector,* Santa Monica, Calif.: RAND Corporation, MG-214-AF, 2004. Online at www.rand.org/pubs/monographs/MG214.

Ausink, John A., Frank Camm, and Charles Cannon, *Performance-Based Contracting in the Air Force: A Report on Experiences in the Field,* Santa Monica, Calif.: RAND Corporation, DB-342-AF, 2001. Online at www.rand.org/pubs/documented_briefings/DB342.

Avery, Susan, "Linking Supply Chains Saves Raytheon $400 Million," *Purchasing,* Vol. 130, No. 16, 2001.

Baldwin, Laura H., John A. Ausink, and Nancy Nicosia, *Air Force Service Procurement: Approaches for Measurement and Management,* Santa Monica, Calif.: RAND Corporation, MG-299-AF, 2005. Online at www.rand.org/pubs/monographs/MG299/.

Baldwin, Laura H., Frank Camm, Edward G. Keating, and Ellen M. Pint, *Incentives to Undertake Sourcing Studies in the Air Force,* Santa Monica, Calif.: RAND Corporation, DB-240-AF, 1998. Online at www.rand.org/pubs/documented_briefings/DB240.

Baldwin, Laura H., Frank Camm, and Nancy Y. Moore, *Strategic Sourcing: Measuring and Managing Performance,* RAND Corporation, DB-287-AF, 2000. Online at www.rand. org/pubs/documented_briefings/DB287.

———, *Federal Contract Bundling: A Framework for Making and Justifying Decisions for Purchased Services,* Santa Monica, Calif.: RAND Corporation, MR-1224-AF, 2001. Online at www.rand. org/pubs/monographs/MR1224.

Burt, David, Donald Dobler, and Stephen L. Starling, *World Class Supply Management: The Key to Supply Chain Management,* 7th ed., New York: McGraw Hill, 2003.

Burt, David, Warren Norquist, and Jimmy Anklesaria, *Zero Base Pricing: Achieving World Class Competitiveness Through Reduced All-In-Costs.* Chicago: Probus, 1990.

Carter, Joseph R., "Development of Supply Strategies," in Joseph Cavinato and Ralph Kauffman, eds., *The Purchasing Handbook,* 6th ed., New York: McGraw-Hill, 1999.

Cox, Andrew, Paul Ireland, Chris Lonsdale, Joe Sanderson, and Glyn Watson, *Supply Chains, Markets and Power: Managing Buyer and Supplier Power Regimes,* New York: Routledge, 2002.

Davies, Jon, "Spare Cash Savings," *Aircraft Economics,* July/August 2004.

Dobler, Donald, and David N. Burt, *Purchasing and Supply Management: Text and Case,* 6th ed., New York: McGraw Hill, 1996.

Ellram, Lisa M., and Thomas Y. Choi, *Supply Management for Value Enhancement: Best Practices in Supply Management,* Tempe, Ariz.: National Association of Purchasing Management, Inc., 2001.

Gabbard, Ernest G., *Strategic Sourcing Critical Elements & Keys to Success,* submitted to the 89th Annual International Supply Management Conference & Educational Exhibit, Philadelphia, Pa., April 2004.

Government Accountability Office, *Acquisition Reform: The Government's Market Research Efforts,* Washington, D.C.: U.S. Government Printing Office, 1996.

Griffith, D., and Lisa M. Ellram, "Managing Small Dollar Purchases," *NAPM InfoEdge,* Vol. 1, No. 7, 1996, p. 5.

"Hackett Report Finds Best Procurement Orgs See Greater ROI," *Purchasing Magazine Online,* December 28, 2005.

Hollingsworth, B., "How to Effectively Rate Your Suppliers," *NAPM InfoEdge,* Vol. 4, No. 3, 1998, p. 8.

Laseter, Timothy M., *Balanced Sourcing: Cooperation and Competition in Supplier Relationships,* San Francisco, Calif.: Booz-Allen and Hamilton Inc., 1998.

Leenders, Michiel R., and David L. Blenkhorn, *Reverse Marketing: The New Buyer-Supplier Relationship,* New York: The Free Press, 1988.

Leenders, Michiel R., Harold E. Fearon, Anna E. Flynn, and P. Fraser Johnson, *Purchasing and Supply Management,* 12th ed., New York: McGraw Hill, 2001.

Monczka, Robert M., Robert J. Trent, and Robert B. Handfield, *Purchasing and Supply Chain Management,* 2nd ed., Cincinnati, Ohio: South-Western, 2002.

Moore, Nancy Y., Laura H. Baldwin, Frank Camm, and Cynthia R. Cook, *Implementing Best Purchasing and Supply Management Practices: Lessons from Innovative Commercial Firms,* Santa Monica, Calif.: RAND Corporation, DB-334-AF, 2002. Online at www.rand.org/pubs/documented_briefings/DB334.

Moore, Nancy Y., Cynthia R. Cook, Clifford Grammich, and Charles Lindenblatt, *Using a Spend Analysis to Help Identify Prospective Air Force Purchasing and Supply Management Initiatives: Summary of Selected Findings,* Santa Monica, Calif.: RAND Corporation, DB-434-AF, 2004. Online at www.rand.org/pubs/documented_briefings/DB434/.

Nordstrom, Richard D., and Richard L. Pinkerton, "Taking Advantage of Internet Sources to Build a Competitive Intelligence System," *Competitive Intelligence Review,* Vol. 10, No. 1, 1999.

Pint, Ellen M., and Laura H. Baldwin, *Strategic Sourcing: Theory and Evidence from Economics and Business Management,* Santa Monica, Calif.: RAND Corporation, MR-865-AF, 1997. Online at www.rand.org/pubs/monograph_reports/MR865.

Porter, Michael E., *Competitive Strategy: Techniques for Analyzing Industries and Competitors,* New York: The Free Press, 1980.

———, *Note on the Structural Analysis of Industries,* Boston, Mass.: Harvard Business School Publishing, 1975, rev. June 30, 1983.

———, *Competitive Advantage: Creating and Sustaining Superior Performance,* New York: The Free Press, 1998.

"Quality Designated as Most Essential Supplier Performance Metric," *Supplier Selection & Management Report,* December 1999.

Raedels, Alan R., *The Supply Management Process: Managing Key Supply Processes,* Tempe, Ariz.: National Association of Purchasing Management, Inc., 2000.

Riggs, David A., and Sharon L. Robbins, *The Executive's Guide to Supply Management Strategies: Building Supply Chain Thinking into All Business Processes,* New York: American Management Association, 1998.

Stundza, Tom, "Ford Shakes Up Its Steel Buy," *Purchasing,* Vol. 130, No. 5, 2001.

Tang, Christopher, "Supplier Relationship Map," *International Journal of Logistics: Research and Applications,* Vol. 2, No. 1, April 1999, pp. 39–56.

U.S. Air Force, *Expeditionary Logistics for the 21st Century Campaign Plan,* Washington, D.C.: Pentagon, April 1, 2005.

U.S. Department of Defense, *SD-2 Buying Commercial & Nondevelopmental Items: A Handbook,* Washington, D.C.: Defense Standardization Program, April 1, 1996. Online at http://www.dsp.dla.mil/documents/sd-2 (as of March 2006).

———, *SD-5 Market Research: Gathering Information About Commercial Products and Services,* Washington, D.C.: Defense Standardization Program, July 1997. Online at http://www.dsp.dla.mil/documents/sd-5/ (as of March 2006).

Younossi, Obaid, Mark V. Arena, Richard M. Moore, Mark A. Lorell, Joanna Mason, John C. Graser, *Military Jet Acquisition: Technology Basics and Cost-Estimating Methodologies,* Santa Monica, Calif.: RAND Corporation, MR-1596-AF, 2003.

Wehr, W. S., "Selecting World Class Distributors: A Case Study," *Proceedings of the 1992 NAPM International Purchasing Conference,* Tempe, Ariz., 1992, pp. 327–332.